何
博
森

THE YEAR I SMELLED LIKE MILK

STORIES FROM BEIJING AND BEYOND

MICHAEL W. HOBSON

Hobson, Michael W.
The year I smelled like milk: stories from Beijing and beyond / Michael W. Hobson.
Includes map and Mandarin glossary.
ISBN 978-0-557-21691-8
1. China – Description and travel – 1993-1994.   2. Beijing (China) – Social life and customs – 1993-1994.

First Edition

Cover and interior design by Michael W. Hobson.
Cover photograph of monk by Chris Orvis; all others by Michael W. Hobson.

theyearismelledlikemilk.wordpress.com

CONTENTS

for my students,
who were the real teachers

and

for my mother,
who crossed the globe to join me

INTRODUCTION

Write what you know, the adage says. Well, I lived in China for a year – I'll write about that. People seem to enjoy those stories almost as much as I enjoy telling them.

The funny thing is, as I wrote I discovered how much I *didn't* know. The background of that holiday. The meaning of those floral displays. The fruit used in those tart candies. How they actually prepared thousand year eggs. Holes in my knowledge urged me to research.

I resisted those urges and left the holes unfilled.

Why?

Plenty of books offer facts about China. Adding another to the market doesn't interest me, because I don't know China from books.

What I do know is this: I lived in China for a year, and it captivated me, bewildered me, amused and frustrated and utterly challenged me. I struggled to comprehend just about every experience. If I wasn't misinterpreting the language, I was missing cultural cues. Asking questions rarely helped; as a foreigner I wasn't privy to complete or straightforward explanations. My

八

hosts tended to put their *best* feet forward.

For me, then, living in Beijing meant passing hourly from one uncertain haze to the next. I arrived with the conviction that all humans are fundamentally the same; I departed with an acquired respect for cultural differences.

So I do not *know* the Chinese; I know only that I spent a year among them, a year that drove me to think a lot about language and culture. This book is my effort to convey how it felt to live in a nation so different from my own, lacking the necessary skills to decode it.

Crazy things happen when cultures collide. I will be just as interested in a Chinese citizen's account of a year in America as I hope you will be in these bemused ramblings.

Timing

I've written my observations in the past tense only, underscoring this book as a memoir. I make no assertions about how China *is* or *isn't*; I only report what I saw, felt and thought while living there from 1993 to 1994.

Which raises the question: why read about China from a prior decade?

Thanks in part to the 2008 Olympics, China is shedding much of its past and solidifying its status as a world leader. Soon we will forget its awkward teenage years, its stumbling, overeager transformation from autocratic excesses to economic powerhouse.

The China I knew stretched between two poles: the political controls of the past and the economic reforms of the future. Street vendors earned more than university professors. Bureaucrats banned firecrackers and pet dogs. Businesses competed through imitation (the communist value of conformity) rather than innovation (the capitalist evil of individualism).

Four years after the Tiananmen Square demonstration, harsh memories interlaced with bright hopes. Looking back on that era is like flipping through a high school yearbook in search of hints about the adults who would emerge – a fascinating exercise.

Language

The glossary at the back should help when you encounter Mandarin words in this book. My general practice is to explain each term upon its first use only. After that I leave you to context, your own memory, and a quick page flip to the rear!

WEBSITE

theyearismelledlikemilk.wordpress.com

THIS WEBSITE OFFERS large, full-color versions of all images, Google Earth placemarkers, video footage, an audible glossary, discussion questions, and links to online articles and resources. It's also a great place to offer feedback, ask questions, and share your own cross-cultural stories.

ACKNOWLEDGMENTS

HOW STRANGE THAT WRITING STARTS OUT isolating, yet in the end involves so many people.

That this book exists at all is a testament to the selflessness of my beloved wife Karyn. I don't think people with young children are meant to write books; the toll this one took on my family was illustrated for me when I once overheard Karyn comparing it to my bout with Lyme disease. Why she would actively enable me to pour so much time into this project is beyond comprehension (it's certainly not from any delusions about royalties!). I love you. Thank you for reading, for listening, for talking through every stage of this project with me, and most of all for giving so much of yourself in pursuit of my dream.

I'm exceedingly grateful to my close friend Reuben Settergren, who kept in regular contact throughout my year in Beijing, and who has now undertaken the journey with me a second time in suggesting revisions. Reuben's uncanny ability to pinpoint the weaknesses in my writing process has rescued this book from more than one quagmire. Thank you for your keen eye and constant friendship.

This book has benefitted immensely from my colleague Augustina Menegay, who helped me render in print form the Mandarin phrases I learned orally. Thank you so much for your assistance, and especially your enthusiasm in what has been a journey of rediscovery for me.

Getting back in touch with biking partners Chris Orvis and Chad was one of this project's highlights. Thank you both for sharing your thoughts on "Journey to the West," and most of all for stretching me beyond myself by including me on that expedition. Chris, thank you also for permitting me to include your fantastic photos.

I've benefitted from correspondence with other colleagues from China, including Nicole Craddock Gulati, Andrea Butler Tian, and Jason S. Wakefield. Each of your paths since that year has been an inspiration. Thank you for your assistance and encouragement.

Donna Kotting graciously read the full manuscript to catch errors my eyes were missing. Thank you for your gift of time and attention.

For a short while pieces of this book lived online, where they received valuable feedback from a number of people including Ellen Hampton Filgo, Donna Kotting, Miranda Winn, Tim Hague, Jasmine Leung, "marcellous," and of course my mother, Anita Hobson. Thank you for your input, and for sharing stories from the wealth of your own cross-cultural experiences.

Additional assistance and encouragement came from Deborah Babcock, Kiersten Bram, Katie Collins, Carol Creed, Barbara Gilmartin, David Hobson, Michael Horrigan, Esther Kim, Sandra Lyons, Theda Mayer, Mary Ellen McNamara, Karen Saunderson, Michelle Shelton, Rich Tyson, Christopher Vee, and Joslyn Wolfe. Thank you for lending your energy and wisdom.

I fear I've left out someone, and for that I apologize.

Of course, as no amount of horses or men could prevent Humpty from falling off the wall, I alone am responsible for the shortcomings that remain in these pages.

My sons, now four and two, have never known a season when Daddy wasn't working on his book. Boys, thank you for being patient with your distracted father. It will be more than a decade before you read these pages, but know this: your responses are the ones I anticipate and will cherish most.

This book concludes with my firstborn, Ben, reflecting on the title. During this conversation my youngest, Alex, not even one at the time, hovered nearby. My wife noticed him hand-signing the word *milk* with some urgency. All that talk about milk was making him thirsty!

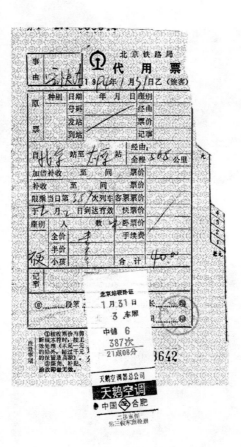

Apartment buildings under construction

Frontispiece

Demolition. Construction. Speeches, posters, TV commercials. She was a city on a mission, boldly trumpeting on a host of banners: "A More Open China Awaits Olympics 2000."

The International Olympic Committee still hadn't selected the site for the Millennium Olympics, and Beijing was gunning for it full force. They'd made it to the final five and viewed competition as a matter of collective desire. A swath of city blocks had been razed to erect an Olympic village of stadiums, apartments, open squares – all eerily vacant, waiting. *China Daily* reported regularly on the status of their bid, the progress of their readiness, the importance of the Olympics to their global position. Once closed to the world, now China sought to play host, laying claim to the status of world leader.

"Do you think Beijing will win?" my students asked, looking to me as their resident authority on matters beyond. Even the waiban, the university liaison for foreign professionals, sought my opinion during a tour of the Olympic village. I was supposed to be impressed. I was supposed to answer that of course Beijing would win, that it simply *had* to based on the excellence of all that had been built, on the immense energy and planning poured into its bid, on the political leaders staking their reputations on victory. The Olympics were China's destiny.

Or were they China's overestimation? Subways and buses were crowded miserably, the airport quaint, the railway station dingy and outdated. I suspected the Olympics were the last thing Beijing's already strained infrastructure could withstand.

But who was I to answer? I knew diddly about hosting a global sports venue.

"Do you think Beijing will win?"

"It looks good," I'd say, "but the other cities also want to win. We'll have to wait and see." A politic answer: why should I take the heat for a rejection I all but knew was coming? Let it land on the heads of the IOC. *They* weren't committed to working in Beijing for a year.

We didn't have to wonder long about the outcome. The decision came September 23, live from Europe. That meant 2:30AM in Beijing, which was no problem – the city was too wired to sleep.

One class of students invited themselves over for my apartment's color TV. We made a party out of it, with snacks, Uno and silly games. Giddy, nervous, they knew that, win or lose, they were about to witness a piece of history.

Around midnight live coverage began: shots of graying Communist Party leaders decked to the hilt, seated before a stage of dancers, acrobats, gymnasts, Beijing opera singers. The entertainment paused between acts for political inspiration, which my students collectively translated:

"This moment is important moment for all of China."

"He says how Olympics are –"

"… complete –"

"… finish –"

"… fulfill the Communist Party goals."

"This is important for the China to show the world how we are –"

"… progress toward global leadership."

At 2:30AM the screen split in half: Chinese politicians on one side, live feed from Europe on the other. An Official Foreign Person stood to hold forth on Olympic heritage, international cooperation, yadda yadda yadda. I couldn't quite make it out beneath the Mandarin interpreter.

Official Foreign Person #2 took the podium. This was the moment.

On screen left, Communist leaders sucked in their breaths. My students sucked in their breaths.

He began simply: "The International Olympic Committee wishes to thank the five bidding cities – Beijing, Berlin, Istanbul, Manchester, and Sydney – for their efforts in presenting their bids."

Only we didn't hear all that, because at the mention of Beijing, China's leaders leapt and cheered! They embraced, slapped each other's backs, tears washing their grinning cheeks.

"Oh no," I groaned.

"Wait," my students said. They looked at me, at each other. "Did he –"

On the TV confetti dropped, music blared. More leaping; more embracing. From the stairwell of my apartment building came muffled shouts from other floors.

Finally my own apartment exploded in laughter and jumping and hugs.

"No no no," I warned, "he hasn't announced the winner." Yet I was one outsider in a small apartment on the north edge of Beijing. Who was I to suggest the leaders of the world's largest nation were wrong?

But wrong they were, and over a language tangle so unfair it was almost a setup. Beijing had come first in an alphabetic list of competitors, so this is what the Chinese heard: "Blah blah blah, blah blah blah blah blah: BeiJING." Even the intonation was correct: in Mandarin *Beijing* is spoken with a low, bouncing tone on *bei* ("north"), then a higher straight tone on *jing* ("city"). Westerners don't say it this way – unless it's in the middle of a list, in which case we raise the pitch on the last syllable to indicate the list will continue. To us, that final high pitch means "Wait, more to come" – but to the Chinese it sounded like the perfect tone for a declaration.

And what a declaration, ringing to reality their most daring dream!

In the midst of all the exuberance something funny happened. Official Foreign Person #2 had continued speaking (had he no tact?), and suddenly the feed from Europe cut to people celebrating in Sydney. Side by side on the screen, Chinese politicians danced beside crowds of ecstatic Australians. Puzzlement crossed my students' faces, then deepened. Something was amiss.

Had those crazy Aussies heard it wrong?

Or …

Reality sagged upon the politicians. In my students, disappointment mixed with embarrassment. They felt misled, cheated, victory ripped from their fingertips by a technicality.

By three o'clock they were trudging back to their dorms in the dark.

The "More Open China" banners still hung in the morning; the announcement must have come too late for workers to get them all. They were removed under the cover of darkness the next night.

Over subsequent days, leaders learned that Beijing had lost by only two votes. They would use this experience as a learning process for their next bid. The world would come to China, they vowed – it was only a matter of time.

Beijing's stadium village remained vacant. No one mentioned the Olympics to me again.

Toll booth on the airport highway :: Hutongs

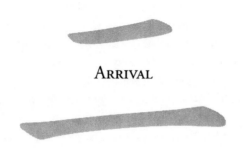

Arrival

Our plane descended in the black night and I thought it strange for an airport to be so far outside the city. Beneath us slept fields, featureless and dark.

Then before the runway swung under us I realized my eyes *weren't* seeing fields. A grid of flattish homes huddled within the darkness, betrayed only by timid candlelight gracing their windowsills. Hutongs.

How long had we coasted above them? Were there really no streetlights? I'd taken the black land for rice paddies.

From the first glimpse Beijing proved even more foreign than I'd hoped.

. . .

I'D SIGNED ON with a Peace Corps-style organization that sent volunteer teachers as a token of cultural exchange. Thirty-eight of us had spent six weeks in Los Angeles for crash courses in culture, Mandarin, and teaching English as a foreign language. We'd bonded in anticipation of our year overseas – a bit of an illusion since we were about to scatter in small teams across a nation roughly the size of the U.S. (*including* Alaska).

We arrived in Beijing a week before fall semester to allow for orientation and rail travel to our destination cities. My teammate Jeff and I were assigned to Beijing and wouldn't need to take a train, which meant more sightseeing for us.

So we thought.

The airport buzzed with checkpoints, stamps and forms – no real lines, just busy counters with uniformed personnel asking questions and scrutinizing IDs. A short gentleman in glasses and a comb over hovered beside us. Eventually Jeff and I realized he wasn't with the airport at all – he was our university's waiban, there to escort us to a waiting taxi. At one in the morning the city streets were still; we ogled the low brick buildings and Chinese signs.

Our driver pulled through a gate into a courtyard filled with parked taxis. Nearby a block-wide construction zone lit the sky, clanking and buzzing into the muggy night air. "Welcome to your new home," our waiban smiled.

"This isn't Youyi (*Friendship*) Hotel?"

"No," he laughed, "you are at Lin Da!" It was the nickname for our university – Beijing Linye Daxue (*Forestry University*), or Lin Da for short.

"Why are there so many taxis?"

"Yes, many taxis," he agreed. "Come!"

We entered the tallest building, five stories, and knocked on a door. Wiry hair and chin stubble poked out, ducked back in, and returned with a fat ring of keys. Our waiban (whose name we'd missed in the airport bustle) introduced him as Xiao Ming, superintendent of the Foreign Experts Guesthouse. Young and wizened, he repeated "Hello" in a manner that suggested it was his only English word. We trooped up four flights of bare concrete steps to receive a quick tour of our apartments: bedroom, kitchen, bathroom, combo living/dining room – each. The tired carpet wasn't padded, the cabinets felt chintzy, yet Jeff and I had expected to share an apartment. By Chinese standards, all this for one person was extravagant.

But weren't we supposed to stay with our fellow teachers at Youyi Hotel? "There's a meeting tomorrow afternoon," I told our waiban. "They want us to be there."

Lin Da entrance (with signage for Beilin Hotel)

"Yes, I know this. A taxi will come tomorrow."

"What time?"

"I'm sorry, at what time is the meeting?"

"Four."

"Yes, a taxi will come at three I think." With a final round of handshakes, Xiao Ming and our waiban left.

Somewhere out in the black night of Beijing, our friends were visiting each other's hotel rooms and comparing first impressions. I wondered if they'd notice our absence.

Meanwhile, we took a wee-morning stroll around the hushed campus, counting every turn so we could retrace our steps. We absorbed the smell of the air, the unfamiliar call of the crickets, the backdrop of construction, and yearned to know what the darkness cloaked around us.

Before turning in I spent several minutes in what would become a bedtime ritual: mosquito squashing. That night I chalked up seven.

. . .

PAST THE CRACKED FIELD BEYOND MY WINDOW, a stream of bicycles, blue trucks and yellow compact vans flowed in two directions, the motion gentle and tiny as a snow globe. I watched until hunger spurred me out of bed.

Nothing in the fridge, cabinets or closets. Just one knife, two glass jars and an iron wok with hints of rust.

I knocked on Jeff's door. No food there. No bottled water either, which was a problem: we'd been warned against drinking unboiled tap water.

Call our waiban? A fine idea, except the phone issued a dead squawk. We were on our own.

View from my apartment

This is pathetic, we thought, boiling water in the rusting wok and then pouring it into glass jars to drink. The first jar cracked when we didn't wait long enough for the water to cool, so we had to share the remaining jar. We boiled a second wokful and left it to cool while we surveyed our surroundings.

The campus looked just as deserted under the glaring sun as it had the night before. Somewhere in Beijing other waibans were escorting our colleagues through world-famous landmarks. We tromped down dusty, isolated streets in search of food.

Without Chinese money we needed a bank, or at least a restaurant that would accept U.S. dollars. After probing several blocks in all directions we found neither – just empty dormitories and classroom buildings, noisy construction, quiet hutongs, and what appeared to be non-university apartments.

Maybe our waiban would call. We returned to our apartments, fussed with the inactive phone. Waited.

At noon our waiban knocked. Accompanying him was a teacher from Lin Da's Foreign Language Department, one of our Chinese counterparts – a slight woman with a loose ponytail and a distinct British accent. They walked us farther from campus than we'd dared, between the skeletal cranes of new construction and down a dust-blown road with electric lines overhead. We entered a restaurant humming with oscillating fans and flies.

Over noodles and stir fry pooled in oil (the more the better, a sign of hospitality), they informed us that Lin Da would remain unpopulated for another week. Until then we were free to explore Beijing on our own. On a napkin our waiban drew a map to a nearby bank where we could exchange money. Instead of renminbi (*people's money*) we would receive Foreign Ex-

*Dusty walk to our
first restaurant*

change Currency (FEC), which we would have trouble spending anywhere but tourist spots. He would check into getting us an advance on our salaries in renminbi. And, he assured, a taxi would pick us up at three for our meeting.

After lunch Jeff and I searched for the bank. Wholly illiterate of even architectural cues, picking the correct building wasn't easy – we blundered into a clothing store and a mom-and-pop version of Kinko's before finding the right one.

They wouldn't exchange our money. Something about missing paperwork.

After a bout of frustrated gestures and loud, slow-mo language, we slunk back to our apartments in defeat, drank the second wok, boiled another.

Three o'clock: no taxi.

And still no phone service. We debated hailing a cab on the street but weren't sure a driver we hired ourselves would accept U.S. dollars. Our decision to wait paid off: half an hour later the university cab arrived.

A full day hadn't passed since our separation from our colleagues, yet it felt like weeks. "Where have you been?" they demanded. Some had seen the Great Wall, others Tiananmen Square and the Forbidden City. Given advances on their salaries, they showed off the souvenirs they'd bought.

"Listen," I implored, pulling two friends aside, "we're going to starve. We've got no money, we can't even exchange it at the bank. Our apartments have no food, we have to boil water in a rusty wok. We can't even get in touch with our waiban – the phone doesn't work and we have no idea where he lives! Is there any way you can lend us some renminbi?"

They graciously handed over two hundred yuan (¥200), enough for a few

Foreign Experts Guesthouse – my apartment was on the fourth floor

kitchen basics and some groceries. Thus armed, Jeff and I returned to Lin Da determined to conquer.

The city wasn't about to go down that easy.

We found Wudaokou, the local market, and bartered for food, only to learn later we were gouged in prices. We ate one meal a day at a restaurant, only to leave hungry after being served dishes like deep fried chicken gristle. Unwilling to fritter our borrowings on taxi fare or risk a bus system we didn't understand, we walked an hour and a half to the Summer Palace, only to be turned away at the gate when they wouldn't accept renminbi from foreigners. Whenever we tried calling our waiban, the phone squawked its line dead tone.

Despite it all, by the end of the week we'd bought a teakettle and several one-liter sodas (I never saw two-liters) so we could use the bottles for storing boiled water. We'd also discovered a government grocery store with fixed prices so we could cook without bankrupting ourselves.

Anything beyond walking radius of Lin Da remained a mystery, but by the time students arrived, springing campus to life, we had duked it out within the tight ring of our surroundings and held our own.

. . .

PEOPLE TENDED TO GRIN when they heard my Chinese name. It sounded considerably grander than the skinny, curly-haired geek in front of them.

Back in Los Angeles I'd been christened at a banquet hosted by the Chinese consulate. Three elderly officials brought us aside in little groups to work on transliterating our American names. Female names tended to con-

Independent sellers' area of Wudaokou market

vey beauty or flowers; male names suggested strength or patriotism. Waiting to receive my own felt a little like standing before Harry Potter's Sorting Hat.

The process of converting English syllables into natural-sounding Chinese took some effort. The officials would debate which sounds and characters to use for each of the three syllables (the standard naming practice), until finally they'd nod and one man would scribble the outcome.

Some disagreement broke out over my name, prompting the gentlemen to glance frequently at me. An apparent flash of inspiration from one brought a flurry of suggestions and smiles from the others. The outcome was scrawled on a Post-it note, and I was named: He Bo Sen.

If you sound it out you'll hear the resemblance to *Hobson*, my last name. The Chinese put their family names first. *He* 何 (pronounced "huh") became mine – a fairly common surname, they said, except that during a whole year in China I didn't meet any other *He*'s. (The character 何 echoed a similar character with the same pronunciation, 河, a homonym that meant "river.")

Bo Sen became my given name. *Bo* 博 (a rhyme of "go") meant "broad" and appeared in the term for Ph.D., suggesting extensive learning. *Sen* 森 fit perfectly – knowing I was headed to Beijing Forestry University, they used the character for "forest."

So there I stood: Broad Forest. (Or, by connotation, River in a Broad Forest.)

Taking on a Native American-sounding name with a flattering meaning seemed kiddish, but this was for real. Immediately I had to practice writing it (my early attempts were shameful) because every form required it: work unit ID, health records, currency exchange log. In the English classroom my

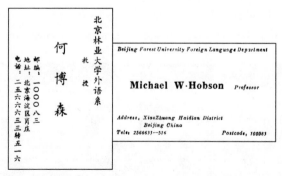

Business cards were duplicated in English on the reverse. Nearly everyone carried cards, which they presented with both hands upon introduction. For fun I chose the vertical format (an older practice) and requested that the numbers be printed in characters, even though the Chinese nearly always used Arabic numerals. Upon receiving my cards I discovered that my students, who'd filled out my order form, had played a joke: they'd promoted me by using the Chinese term for "professor."

students referred to me as "Mistah Hobison." Everywhere else I was either He Bo Sen or He Laoshi (*Teacher He*).

. . .

Pointing at a pile of eggs, I'd ask, "Zhe ge duo shao qian (*How much does this cost*)?"

"Ba mao."

I'd stand there counting up to ba (*eight*), then say, "Tai gui le (*How expensive*)!"

"Liu mao."

Mental counting (yi, er, san, si, wu, liu = *six*), then a smile: "Yao (*I want*)." The vendor would weigh several eggs in a metal basket and report the price. I'd pay, he'd pile them in a plastic bag to hand over, and I'd leave the transaction proud.

Proud, that is, until weeks later, when students informed me the going rate for eggs was two mao (*dimes*) per gram, not six. That was pretty much the rule until I wised up: the white guy with the big nose pays three times as much. No wonder they called me from stall to stall to show off their wares. Foreigners made great customers.

I became a tougher sell after that. Earning a stipend of just $100 U.S. a month, I felt I had to.

In addition to the stipend I earned eight hundred yuan monthly – considerably higher than the average professor's salary (¥350), higher even the typical street seller's income (¥400-500). Still, I fretted over the low stipend and saved some yuan to convert and take back home. Consequently Wudaokou vendors found me a jackrabbit, ready to flee at the slightest suspicion.

Early on I didn't even earn Chinese money, technically. Only citizens of the People's Republic of China could use renminbi. Foreigners used Foreign

Wudaokou market

Exchange Currency (FEC), a parallel system that exchanged at a weaker rate, giving it less buying power. While most renminbi bills were rumpled, FEC stayed in near-mint condition from lack of use. Government stores accepted FEC, but street vendors couldn't be bothered. The trick was to break a large FEC bill at a government store and beg for the change in renminbi.

A few months into the year China abandoned FEC. How long had FEC been in place? What prompted the change? I didn't know, but the switch caused instant inflation. My weekly jar of peanut butter rose from eight yuan to twelve; other prices followed suit. My salary increased as well, from ¥800 to ¥1310. I assumed Chinese salaries were also raised.

No longer was I treated as a foreigner in every financial transaction. No longer was I asked for my work unit card to prove my right to make and spend the same money as everyone else. Such principles are a given in America, but for the Chinese, granting foreigners direct access to their economy must have seemed an immense risk.

Unlike U.S. dollar bills, Chinese yuan varied in size and color and were emblazoned with anonymous citizens, idealized portraits of both women and men, dashing and energetic with their strong jaws and wide foreheads. Minority groups were represented through variations in clothing and facial features, as well as a few lines in other writing systems. Only the largest bill, ¥100, abandoned commoners to depict Communist Party leaders. I admired these bills both for their beauty and their technical superiority – American dollars didn't catch up with watermarks and color microprint until two years later.

Most Chinese coins, however, were flimsy as tin. On a hunch I used pliers to dangle one over the gas range in my kitchen. Within a minute it warmed to red, then became a glowing white goop that slouched like a water balloon. A second later it dropped to the tile floor and splattered into a

Renminbi bills: one, two, and one hundred (high denominations were larger in size)

25

Rorschach blot.

. . .

WALK IN, PICK A TABLE. When the waitress welcomes you, request a drink: "Qing gei wo shui (*Please give me water*)."

Now point anywhere on the Chinese-only menu. Illiteracy makes dining out fun! Sometimes you get stir-fried shrimp, sometimes you get sea slug. No matter what, take a nibble – for manners, but primarily for bragging rights.

Once Jeff and I received the dilemma of a cooked fish, lips to tail. How does one consume a whole fish without fork or knife? We must have looked silly huddled over the plate, Jeff using his chopsticks to steady the fish while I excavated beneath the scales.

Near the end of that first week I stumbled on one entrée I loved, and asked the waitress to repeat its name so I could practice it. At restaurants thereafter, better safe than hungry, I ordered gong bao ji ding: stir-fried chicken with peanuts and vegetables. Nothing fancy, but definitely a tummy pleaser.

I ate a lot of gong bao ji ding that year.

. . .

BEIJING LINYE DAXUE owned and operated a hotel. And a taxi fleet. And a gas station. Services for faculty and students? Hardly – they were pitched at the public.

The university had capital; why not use it to bring in extra revenue? Wasn't that what capitalism – no, a "socialist market economy with Chinese characteristics" – was all about? For a successful model they needed look no

Renminbi bills: five, ten, and fifty

further than American college sports.

Midway through the year Lin Da began renovating vacant apartments in the Foreign Experts Guesthouse. They also contracted fewer foreign instructors. Leasing units to outsiders had proven lucrative.

Side businesses also provided perks, reflecting the Chinese principle of guanxi: whoever had the pull got the favors. University officials enjoyed owning a hotel to accommodate visiting family and friends. Who *wouldn't* want their own taxi fleet for easy transport around the city? And if they took the university car for a spin, their own gas station could fill it for free.

Best of all, access to such services put officials in the position of granting favors to others, amassing yet more guanxi for themselves.

. . .

A TEAM OF FELLOW TEACHERS lived less than a mile away. At our Youyi Hotel meeting they'd loaned me money and had given me their phone number. I didn't know my own number, so it was up to me to call.

Unfortunately I still wasn't getting a dial tone. I mentioned this three times to Xiao Ming, the building superintendent, only to be told repeatedly my phone was fine.

It wasn't. Day after day it emitted the same dispiriting squawk.

One day, on a lark, I dialed my friends' number anyway.

It worked! I never guessed China's dial tone would sound different.

Next came a low beeping. Was that ringing? A busy signal? How long should I listen? I felt sheepish being unable to figure out something as simple as a phone!

Beilin ("North Forest," a variant of Beijing Linye) Hotel with taxi fleet

Thankfully I didn't have to wait long. The line clicked harshly and a woman answered, "Wei!" (*Hello*, used only when answering the phone).

I didn't expect a human operator, but it made sense – my friends' number included an extension. This was the moment of truth for my fledgling Mandarin: could I communicate without facial expressions or hand gestures? I inhaled, then pronounced, "San ling san ling (*Three zero three zero*)."

"Shen me (*What*)?"

A little louder, a little clearer: "San ling san ling."

"Shen me?" An additional flurry of words flew across the line.

Again, clownishly articulate: "San ling san ling."

She had no clue what I was saying.

The next day, after a language brainstorm, I tried again: "Qing gei wo san ling san ling (*Please give me three zero three zero*)."

"Shen me?"

Sigh. Louder, slower: "Qing gei wo san ling san ling!"

Word flurry.

Typically I preplanned my every attempt at Mandarin through some vigorous mental rehearsal, but desperation inspired an improvised plea for mercy: "Wo shi Meiguoren (*I am an American*). Qing gei wo san ling san ling."

No go.

Every day I tried, hoping for a different operator. Every day the same voice answered, wondering why this strange foreigner insisted on bleating gibberish in her ear.

Weeks later I was perusing a traveler's dictionary when I came across the phrase *qing zhuan*. Translation? "Please transfer …"

I dialed again and spoke, "Qing zhuan san ling san ling."

"Oh!" she answered. The line clicked, and there was Chuck.

"We've been worried about you!" he scolded. "Why didn't you call?"

. . .

I'D FOLLOWED THE RULES: tuberculosis inoculation within six months of arrival. Unbeknownst to me the requirement had changed, tightening the window to three months. My shot missed the new mark by two weeks.

The waiban had driven me to a hospital to validate my health records when the discrepancy was discovered. I needed another inoculation. Right then.

I'd read about Chinese hospitals. They didn't always use clean needles, and despite government denials, AIDS was a growing problem. I'd followed the rules; I didn't want a shot. I told my waiban this. He returned to the little window in the wall to see what could be done. After a while he forced his way through the crowd to a second little window.

They kept passing him between the two windows. With each switch he whispered a progress report – "I think maybe this time yes" – that sounded progressively more like the Chinese reluctance to give a flat-out no. An hour later he returned my records to me.

I needed the shot.

Scrutinizing my immunization form for a loophole, I glared at the offending date: May 8. Why hadn't I procrastinated? The same day in June would've been fine.

It occurred to me then just how similar May and June looked in numeric form: 5, 6.

My pen hovered over the month figure, highlighting this irony with an angry pantomime of the simple stroke it would take. To my surprise the waiban said, "Yes, I think this is a good idea," as if he'd been wondering why I hadn't reached this conclusion sooner (thus sparing him the runaround).

Would it be illegal? Would I get caught? Deported?

I *really* didn't want that shot.

So with a skill born of urgency (plus a few trial runs on a scratch sheet), I doctored the form, he brought it back to the window, and the clerk stamped it. I was legit.

How that clerk failed to recognize the forgery mystified me. She'd already seen my shot record several times, looking at the precise date in question.

As we exited the hospital I wondered if I'd stumbled upon the Chinese method of dealing with red tape.

. . .

AT THE BUS STOP: "Lao Wai."

Across the restaurant: "Lao Wai."

From bicycles whizzing by as I waited for a bus, the second syllable softer, Doppler-style: "Lao Wai."

I heard it around campus, in the subway, on packed sidewalks like a squeak in my shoes. No one said it to my face; they only muttered the incantation as they passed, as if blessing me after a sneeze: "Lao Wai."

Students told me it meant "Uncle Outsider." *Wai* was used in *waiguoren* ("foreigner") and *waiban* ("liaison who helps foreigners"). *Lao*, a family term, came from the singsong rhyme "Lao Wai hen qi guai (*Uncle Outsider very strange*)." About one in fifty people muttered "Lao Wai" upon sighting me; periodically, perhaps twice a month, I was treated to the whole refrain.

Smaller towns and villages unaccustomed to foreigners yielded higher rates.

Americans admonish children for staring at anyone who appears unusual. A few Chinese parents actually pointed me out. Even some adults indulged in unabashed staring. Among such an immense population they weren't likely to see me again, so they got in their looks while they could.

As we walk through life we make impressions on others constantly, unavoidably, impressions that escape us because they're rarely (if ever) voiced. So I found it quite odd to receive regular feedback on my presence as though I were some minor celebrity.

. . .

HOW COULD A CITY SO NEAR THE DESERT – the great Gobi, of *Flight of the Phoenix* fame – be ridden with mosquitoes? The netting I'd hoisted over my bed was far from impregnable, so the evening squash sessions continued. My bedtime kill record: twelve.

Beetles and moths, bees and roaches fascinated me. They weren't exotic in any safari sense, but subtle differences in color and shape underscored my global displacement. Wishing I could share these discoveries with friends back home, I scooped samples into a plastic cup and transferred them to a Ziploc bag for starvation and mummification. Before long this collection included twenty unique specimens. Would I be able to sneak such a bag through customs? Would doing so kick off an intercontinental pandemic?

Questions like these didn't bother me – the collecting was fun.

Eventually I managed to snare what I'd dubbed a Terminator Wasp. By "managed" I mean "screwed up enough courage," because the beast was double the largest wasp I'd seen in America. At that size its black, segmented features resembled the monster in the film *Alien*. Every time one of these predators entered my screenless windows, I cowered.

Gradually I made some timid swipes with a cup until one day, by blind luck I'm sure, I trapped one. In the Ziploc its jagged appendages probed relentlessly for an escape, prompting me to check and recheck the bag's seal.

When I returned from dinner it was gone – chewed a hole straight through. As a farewell courtesy it had ripped to pieces all my other insects, leaving behind a tossed salad of wings and thoraces and antennae.

This concluded my entomological pursuits.

. . .

FIRST AND FOREMOST, they were *bicycles*, not bikes. Upright, grandfatherly, they were the black steel Oldsmobiles of the cycling world. Bell on handlebars. Single gear. Two-spring seat. Rear carry rack.

Second, the video footage I'd seen didn't begin to paint the picture: bicycles were *everywhere*.

Two kinds, personal or truck. Technically the trucks were tricycles, one front wheel for steering, a platform on two oversized wheels behind. Wide as a kitchen table, these platforms could support stacks of chicken crates or vegetable boxes or lumber higher than the bicyclist's head. Consequently truck bicycles moved slower, riders pumping at the extended chain stretching back to the rear axle.

Personal bicycles weren't a whole lot faster. Thanks in part to an economy lacking in rewards for speed or initiative, people cycled as though every trip were a stately outing. This was also defensive: a slow speed allowed a quicker stop when drivers darted through bicycle lanes (right of way belonging to the mode of transport less likely to sustain damage). Mostly, however, casual pedaling seemed a function of a relaxed mindset.

As an American I had trouble adjusting. I typically wound left and right through slower traffic: an aggressive bicyclist.

Learning to ride was a significant rite of passage (imagine if American children earned their cultural badge of independence, driving, at age five or six). Another rite was having a bicycle stolen; some of my students had lost two or three. A steel ring bolted to the frame clicked around the rear tire, blocking the spokes from spinning, but that didn't prevent someone from carrying away the entire bicycle.

Safety, then, lay in numbers. Bicycles could be parked anywhere, but a loner invited temptation. It was worth the longer walk to find a bicycle

Bicycle traffic near Wudaokou

parking lot – a designated area attended by a woman with an armband who collected a few mao for her service. Finding your black steel bicycle among dozens of other black steel bicycles could be a challenge. I looked for the peeling yellow sticker beneath my seat, then verified by the pattern of paint scratches on my handlebars.

Waves of bicycles created a constant demand for repairs. There was no shortage of repairmen, who could set up shop on any corner with one crate of tools and supplies, and a second to sit on. My preferred mechanic was Yang Jin Yu, an older gentleman who serviced student and staff bicycles from an open-air shop on campus. Frequently one of my pedals would flop around or my handlebars would droop, giving me reason to stop by his shop practically every month. I was one of Yang's regulars, the cheapskate American who'd bought a worn out steed at only ¥111. He treated me like family and exhibited more patience with my stilted Mandarin than anyone else I knew. And he never accepted payment from me, no matter how I tried to press money into his hand or slip it into his tool crate.

. . .

THE RETIRED CHAIR of Lin Da's Foreign Language Department, a professor emeritus who still lived on campus, was 76. Every Saturday morning he hopped on his bicycle and pedaled to Tiananmen Square and back, three hours round trip.

I didn't know a single American that age who could *balance* on a bicycle.

Rarely did I see overweight people in China, or even stocky people. This must have been due in part to daily walking and cycling. It was practically unheard of for an individual to own a car, and taxi costs added up.

Rite of passage

Often groups of friends or coworkers cycled together. A husband might pedal with his wife seated sideways across the rear rack, shoulders leaning over one side, feet dangling shy of the spokes on the other. Sometimes the wife also carried a small child – an entire family on one bicycle. Later in the year, when my mother visited, I tried pedaling with her on the back. It was awkward at first, but we got the hang of it.

Occasionally I witnessed one person riding two bicycles: sitting on one while reaching over to steer the other. Perhaps a friend had been dropped off at the railway station, or a husband had picked up his wife's bicycle from the repair shop. I tried this stunt too, with little success.

The Chinese were so comfortable on bicycle I wished I could try an experiment: line up forty people around the perimeter of a football field, and direct each person to cross to a position diagonally opposite, everyone starting simultaneously. In walking toward their destinations, all forty would converge near the center of the field, where they would need to alter path and pace to avoid collision. Not very difficult – any set of forty people could manage it on foot.

But I believed the Chinese would also manage it on bicycle.

. . .

I'D EXPECTED CHINA TO BURST FORTH in Technicolor like a vibrant, gong-clanging, headdress-wearing dragon dance. Instead Beijing's colors were gray and brown, its predominant sound the drone of traffic.

I worried about the sky. A few days that year it cleared to a pale blue; climbing the gang ladder to the roof of my building I could see the mountain range silhouetted to the north. All other days, week upon week, a dusty

At Xizhimen intersection, a circle within a circle: one overpass for cars, the other for bicycles

smoggish soup choked the atmosphere, flattening vision in a bland smear from asphalt to buildings to sky. Exhaust stained the backs of buses, trucks; I wondered if a year in Beijing would stain my lungs.

A dozen smokestacks stabbed upward from the blocks surrounding my apartment. Inactive during the day, after dusk they turned adamant, spewing thick fumes as if racing against dawn. It seemed like an environmental version of saving face, paying lip service by sweeping pollution under the rug of darkness. At nights I lay on my stiff mattress thinking about the toxic recipe being concocted for our morning air. American cities may not be much better – I've seen the grunge-bubble of New York City from 30,000 feet – but something about the frenzy of those midnight smokestacks, right within city limits, made Beijing's pollution seem unchecked.

What struck me most about the sky, though, was the lightning.

In America, lighting looks bluish purple and tends to branch downward. The lightning I saw in Beijing seemed to be tinted orange and tended to arc in webs from cloud to cloud.

I didn't see many storms that year; perhaps this impression formed from too few samples to be accurate. But my sincere, slack-jawed sense was that the lightning looked different, utterly foreign – and somehow *Chinese*, as if even electricity were a cultural construct.

. . .

NO, I DIDN'T FIND surveillance bugs in my apartment.

Yes, I did search. This was Communist China after all, Tiananmen

Approaching dust storm from the nearby Gobi Desert, 5PM – an eerie event of yellows and grays, misplaced shadows, wind and dust and tinkling glass

Square China. Who better to monitor than a young American sure to be a CIA operative? Not finding hidden mics was mild reassurance for an espionage novice like myself, so I kept a tight rein on discussions of politics and religion.

Uncertainty about people listening in took some getting used to. Fellow teachers and I staged mock conversations about how fabulously wealthy we were, about the dozens of countries we'd visited, about our pet pigs and monkeys back home. In reality, though, Lin Da had a reputation for being sui bian (*relaxed*). Most buildings required visitors to register, but not mine – so when friends, or even friends of friends, from other cities visited Beijing they often stayed with us. We weren't up to anything; the thought of surveillance simply was that uncomfortable.

Some monitoring was matter-of-fact. Routinely I received my mail opened. To make any long distance call I had to register my name along with the phone number and name of the person I was calling (standard practice in China). I wasn't allowed to use a photocopier; if I needed worksheets for my students I had to ask the department secretary, who always made two extra copies to keep. I supposed one stayed on file so the department could track my lessons. Who kept the other copy?

This arrangement was so slow – usually copies took days to arrive in my box, thwarting planned lessons – that I began frequenting the mom-and-pop print shop I'd discovered the first day. Yet even there customers had to register, weren't allowed to operate the machines themselves ... and the store filed an extra copy.

A few incidents felt too deliberate to be accidents, like when I visited Tiananmen Square with a video camera. Visitors scattered widely across the paved expanse, yet a woman untangling a kite with her daughter edged to three feet behind me, within easy earshot of my narration into the camera. I noticed her shadow next to mine and jolted, afraid she'd overheard me mention 1989.

Might some of my own students have been informants? Several were card-carrying Party members. That an agent might tap them for information about me wasn't farfetched.

That possibility made me weigh the impact of every word I spoke.

Campus organizations recruit new students

UNIVERSITY

One by one they squirmed. For many I was the first American they'd met. Hearts in throats, they sat in the plush chair and told me their names and hometowns: Taiyuan in Shanxi Province, Changsha in Hunan Province. I, in turn, pretended to recognize these places – the equivalent of a tourist in America feigning familiarity with places like Colorado or Detroit.

As I assessed each student's English proficiency I'd smile and nod, they'd smile and nod, and sometimes that would be the gist. One woman with low skills and nervous hands mentioned that her hobby was origami. Hoping to dispel our verbal awkwardness, I asked her to demonstrate. Little did I guess how difficult origami would be with quivering hands (and, considering the flapping of the paper in the otherwise silent room, how noisy).

A few students explained why they wanted to learn English by recounting sad stories of meeting foreigners but being unable to communicate. I couldn't help contrasting their attitude with America's of expecting others to learn *our* language.

Nearly all students were older than me. Many hoped to study abroad and had registered to take the GRE. I felt daunted for them: the GRE was tough enough without taking it in a foreign language.

Some pointed on a wall map to show how far they'd traveled for this program – in some cases over 24 hours by train, leaving spouse and child to live for a semester in a cramped dormitory with poor heating and no air conditioning. Assigned three or four to a room, they ate bland cafeteria food and shared one phone in the dorm lobby. Such sacrifices inspired me to work overtime to help them learn.

I didn't enjoy spotlighting them in one-on-one interviews, but I needed to evaluate their fluency. They'd taken English since grade school, but head knowledge didn't automatically convert into real-world conversation. What did English *really* sound like? Despite their nerves, a few exhibited eagerly and well. Others, baffled by my questions, shook their heads with uncomfortable grins and said nothing. Many interchanges occurred along these lines:

"How are you?"

"Twenty-six."

"Where do you work?"

"Yes."

One woman kept repeating, "I'm sorry, I can't stand you" (instead of *understand*).

I combined these interviews with a written test to divide them into three sections. Those in the lower two sections took their placement as a loss of face, yet their responses couldn't have differed more. The bottom class approached learning with a sense of humor; since their English was poorest they had nothing to lose. But the middle group, expecting a higher placement, soured. No one in this section owned up to having an English name, a standard practice for language learners, and none would accept one. Few participated actively; often they skipped homework. While the upper and lower sections warmed up quickly, this middle group seemed to want to develop conversation skills through silent sitting.

So I wasn't surprised when the lowest section began to surpass the middle. With nowhere to go but up, they'd participated freely for the sheer silly joy of learning a language, consequently growing by bounds.

*Foreign Languages
Building*

Among this group an inspirational story unfolded in the form of Tracy, a nineteen-year-old who'd slipped through grade school with practically no English. Recently hired as a secretary, Tracy floundered through the first weeks of our immersion class and needed to be carried along with extra tutoring. About a month into the semester, however, I caught her repeating a tricky word with a clean accent.

I pointed her out to the class. "Please say that again, Tracy. You see? Say it like she does." Modeled after my native accent, her pronunciation trumped that of her book-learned classmates. By the end of the semester her vocabulary still lagged, but she could pass herself off with the most natural-sounding speech of them all.

. . .

THE FIRST MORNING OF CLASS was over. I packed my teaching bag. Students watched.

"We're finished," I reiterated.

No one budged.

"You can go to lunch now," I encouraged. "Please, don't wait for me. You're free to go."

Smiling politely, they remained in their seats.

It took me a minute to collect everything, hurrying as they watched. I'd heard of this, but that didn't make organizing my papers under sixteen gazes less unsettling. They were hungry; they would be late to the canteen. Still they waited. Finally I slung my bag over my shoulder, hefted my teaching crate and stepped out the door.

Like a choral exhale they stood, filing out after me.

We repeated this exercise at the end of day two.

Practicing street directions

And at the end of day three, at which point I yelped, "Enough of this! I'm an American teacher. This is an English class. Everyone stand up. Stand up. Come on, I'm serious! Up! Now – everyone out the door. Yes, yes, out. Go on out. This is how it works in America. Good job! Have a great lunch."

The fourth day it took a little coaxing, but they shuffled out before me without a scene.

Friday they needed no coaxing at all, just waltzed out, smiles and chatter, like pros.

Suddenly I missed it. That little show of respect, though awkward, had been affirming – yet I'd gone and blustered it away. Shouldn't it have taken them longer to adjust? Maybe waiting for the teacher was a formality they would just as soon drop. Or what if (gulp) they found it easy to walk out on me due to some lack of respect?

Rather than prove myself a cool American, I wondered if I'd cast off a bond of esteem.

. . .

TWO THOUSAND UNDERGRADS at Beijing Linye Daxue, six hundred grads, and several dozen professionals on campus for immersive English training. Generally my students' ages ranged between 22 and 35; a few professionals were in their forties, two in their fifties.

Classrooms had concrete floors and cinder block walls painted in a color scheme repeated throughout the nation: pale green below the waist, white up to the ceiling. The walls were dusty, the paint so cracked it snapped away if we taped anything to it. Desks lined the perimeter of the room, leaving the

Lin Da main gate

middle empty. Women tended to sit on one side, men on the other.

At the beginning of each class I erased the whiteboard, tested my fading markers, and called roll (tricky at first for the section that declined English names). Teaching meant getting them to talk, which wasn't easy – most played shy. Over time, however, many developed into regular chatterboxes.

"Any questions?" I asked at the end of every class. Rarely did anyone respond. Only after dismissal would a few individuals come up with questions they were reluctant to ask in front of their peers.

I taught three sections of graduate students who needed foreign language credits, and one section of professionals who needed English for their careers. Teachers rotated between classrooms while students stayed put, an arrangement that cast the teacher as interloper. In America, random students assemble for a short time on the teacher's turf in a room customized for the subject; in China the teacher stepped into *their* turf, with the only learning materials those carried in.

Offsetting this home field advantage was a Confucian heritage of respect for authority (a cultural trait conveniently tapped to reinforce one-party government). Student deference did wonders to smooth out the weaker aspects of my teaching; any remaining awkwardness was siphoned off by the class leader.

When and how did a section select its leader? I never knew, but the position helped the learning dynamic immensely. A face-saving intermediary, the leader voiced concerns to the teacher. If students were displeased by the amount of homework or needed a slower pace, rather than stew about it they told the leader, who presented the matter in private. Better yet, the leader

In the classroom – I'm the waiguoren on the left
(the mustache was an attempt to appear older)

could advise the teacher on appropriate responses, and even screened out trivial complaints by telling classmates they were whining.

Despite the title, a class leader didn't necessarily make decisions – that power remained with the collective. They deliberated over even trivial things: not only when to visit the Summer Palace, but which bus to take. Americans tend to prove their worth by contributing the brightest ideas; my students seemed more eager to elicit others' ideas, and to conspicuously subordinate their own desires to group consensus.

This profoundly *corporate* attitude (no doubt the product of Communist training) amazed me. On top of meeting together for six hours of class each day, they shared dorm rooms, in different buildings by gender. Under such conditions most Americans would seek alone time, but my students ate in the canteen together, played sports together, went on weekend excursions together – if not as an entire class, at least with subgroups.

So I was surprised when, during the spring semester, a young woman named Teresa began lingering in the classroom after dismissal. She made a ruse of needing to talk to me, but this continued day after day, and she seemed forlorn. I noticed her eating alone in the canteen, and when her classmates came to my apartment for evening Free Talks she no longer joined them.

At the beginning of the term Teresa had been symbiotically bonded to classmate Emily. Then one day she simply sat at the opposite end of the room and avoided eye contact.

Why the pariah treatment? I asked the class leader, who merely responded "It is complicated" with an expression that suggested I was overstepping my bounds. To this day I have no idea what, within so group-oriented a culture, could have estranged Teresa so suddenly from her peers.

In my memory her exile lasted the rest of the semester, but in a photograph from our farewell karaoke party she is there, sitting in a plush chair, smiling at one of the more cheerful men talking with her. I'm glad for this evidence, because all I remember is the awfulness of seeing her alone day after day, separated from her friends, away from home and family, looking utterly afflicted.

. . .

MOST USED ENGLISH NAMES: Johnny, Heather, Rick, Sarah, Matt, Rebecca.
Some of those aliases were unusual: Rhea, Tiger, Flower, Rainy, Music.
"Wait right there," I objected. "You can't call yourself *Music*."
"Yes, this is my English name."

"No, it can't be. *Music* isn't a name. Does your Chinese name mean *music*?"

"No, but I like music you see, so I choose it." He was so insistent I left it alone – and later came to love it. For someone so kind-spirited, so perpetually ready to laugh with his classmates, the name fit.

Three girls came with inadvertently suggestive names, though I didn't know how to tell them: Honey, Jelly and Cherry. "Those words can't be names."

"Why not?"

Imagining them arriving in America for graduate studies, I said, "They just can't" – a prim answer that failed to dissuade them from years of identification with sweet condiments. These names also stayed.

. . .

COMPOSITION: DESCRIBE YOUR FAMILY.

> *My home is in the Hang-Jia-Hu plain, Zhejiang province. The plain is known as the land of fish and rice and abound with silk.*
>
> *There are five members in my family. They are my parents, my brother and his wife and my brother's son. My family live in the countryside and are all peasants. My parents farm for the whole life, while my brother and his wife are workers in factories managed by the collective.*
>
> *In the countryside there are so much farm work that my family are very busy all the year. As other peasants do there, my parents plant double-crop rice. In winter they raise wheat and rapeseed. They also take up silkworm breeding. In addition, my family has a small fish farm and some sheep. So my parents have to cut grass to feed them every day.*
>
> *My family are very busy all the time, but we are still poor. The main reason is that the agro chemicals and fertilizer are too much expensive. 50kg unhusked rice is even cheaper than one bottle of agro chemicals. Although this year the government raised the price of unhusked rice it doesn't change the situation greatly.*

. . .

ON THE BUS TO YIHE YUAN (*the Summer Palace*) my students grinned, chatted, laughed. They'd invited me along for some weekend sightseeing. I supposed playing tour guide for the foreign teacher was fun, but it didn't explain why they bristled with such excitement.

Then we entered the park grounds and the reason became clear: Yihe

Yuan was as new to them as it was to me. Most had never visited Beijing before – in fact I'd been in the city longer than they had, by one week. While I appreciated some nifty architecture, they were touching their own history.

My students came from a variety of cities, some a good stretch of continent away. The few Beijing natives among them were both ribbed and envied for their putonghua (*standard speech*), with its words ending in extra R's ("duor" instead of "duo," similar to the British "idear"). They cackled at each other's variant pronunciations, and since the only Mandarin I learned came from Beijing they delighted in my "proper" accent, marveling, "You speak better Chinese than me!"

Northerners, who ate mainly noodles and diced meats and vegetables, teased southerners about their cuisine of more exotic species and organs. This regional difference came into play at a restaurant where students gave me an impromptu lesson in dissection.

It was the same dilemma as before: fish served whole, to be consumed with chopsticks. I still had no clue how to proceed with dignity.

"Look, pick it up like this," they said, pinching chopsticks around the fish's middle. "Then bite here and remove this bone" – into the back, pulling out the fin rays – "and now you can eat the meat. Then turn it over" – laying it on the plate, then lifting from the opposite side – "bite out this bone" – the spine – "and eat here."

I can be a squeamish eater, but this process was so biologically precise and self-reliant that I couldn't resist following it step by step. At the end of the meal we each had a fish head and tail on the plate.

"You don't eat the head?" I teased.

"No no no," they protested – all except Matt, from the southern city of Changsha, who boasted, "Sure!"

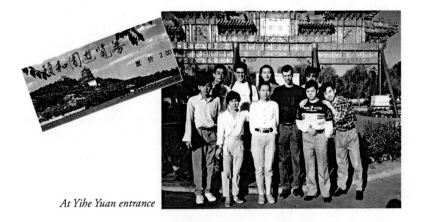

At Yihe Yuan entrance

"Oh yes," they remembered, "Matt will eat it! In the south they eat things like this."

"Eat it, Matt!"

Happy to oblige, Matt lifted his fish head in his chopsticks, spine and tail dangling, and brought it close to his mouth. Eyeing us mischievously, he drew the head in close, kissed it on the lips – then popped it inside, eyeballs and all, chomping it off at the spine.

"Eww!" we grimaced in unison, Chinese and American alike.

Ordinarily they spat out the bones. Mike, too much the showman for that, ground them up and swallowed the entire mass in one gulp, opening his mouth and waggling his tongue as proof.

. . .

WALKING THROUGH YIHE YUAN, my students twittered over an information placard. Emily translated: "It says the men who served the emperor, they removed six organs."

I knew Chinese emperors had permitted only eunuchs to serve them in order to safeguard their wives and concubines. What I didn't know was about the, err, eunuchification process – precisely what was removed, how, and to what effects. Learning that the process involved so many organs astonished me. "Are you joking?" I asked. "Six organs?"

"Yes," she laughed. "They removed six organs."

Quick mental tally: two male orbs, appendix, one kidney … perhaps the gall bladder? I was coming up short. "That doesn't make sense," I said. "You can't live without six organs."

Emily giggled again. They were all giggling. "Yes! It is quite easy to live without six organs I think. All of the men had them removed."

Yihe Yuan

"No," I protested, "there's *no way* you can live without six organs. It's impossible." Everyone was laughing and blushing. There was a mystery here, some inside joke I wasn't getting, and I wanted to understand. "Tell me which ones they removed."

She bit her lip. Maybe she didn't know the English terms for internal organs? "Okay, the kidney," I said, pointing at the small of my back. Everyone exploded with guffaws. "The appendix," I continued, taking a guess beneath my rib cage. "What else?"

Less laughter now; everyone blushed furiously. Emily looked trapped, even pained, which confused me – she only had to point. Instead she looked away and objected, "But I already told you, they removed six organs –"

Finally I got it: *sex* organs.

· · ·

COMPOSITION: DESCRIBE A CHILDHOOD MEMORY.

> *Countryside born and countryside bred, I had a happy childhood. In my memories, one of my favorite childhood things is that I was always the leader of a band of boys (or my playfellows). Sometimes we put on plays, which produced by we naughty boys. I was the director and I cast everyone in a role.*
>
> *Sometimes we were a band of soldier. I was the commander. I ordered them to fight fire and we defeated the enemy and my soldiers cheered around me.*

· · ·

MISTAH HOBISON, what is a UFO?"

"Mistah Hobison, do you think Chinese girls are more beautiful than

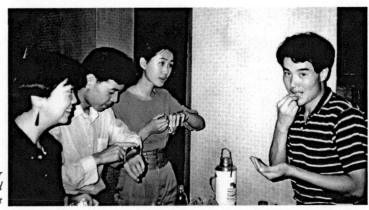

Sunflower seed contest

American girls?"

"Mistah Hobison, can you breakdance?"

This was Free Talk. Four evenings a week I opened my apartment for students to drop in. The intent was informal English practice, but these gatherings quickly shifted to an English/Mandarin blend.

As a host I stocked up on peanuts, crackers, sunflower seeds, tangy fruit candies, cookies and grapes. We played games: Hearts, Mahjong, and Uno with all the house rules thrown in. They loved Bippity Bop Bop Bop, a silly call and response game I taught them, only they changed the name to Bippity But But But because repeating "bop bop" sounded to them like *baba*, the Mandarin word for "father" – and calling each other a name ordinarily reserved for respect weirded them out.

They asked about Dracula, Big Foot, Madonna. They wanted to know about crime in America, how dangerous our streets were, how we rehabilitated convicts. They asked how our married couples meet, and told me that in China it was illegal for women to marry before the age of 23, men before 25. They said their work units would select spouses for them. They wanted to know about American universities, and told me their majors had been decided for them by test score. My graduate students had all scored the exact same percentage, which designated them forestry majors. One point higher would have turned them into architects; students with still higher scores became doctors and scientists.

I never knew quite how to take these revelations. Thanks to language difficulties and my incomplete grasp of social institutions, I feared the impressions their words created in my mind were so incomplete as to constitute *mis*information.

Their favorite question: how was I coping with culture shock? They'd

Uno (an instant favorite) became rowdy enough that we ditched the table and sat on the floor – rather unusual as the Chinese didn't consider floors clean enough for sitting

all heard of this phenomenon (perhaps because many planned to study over-seas), so I served as their test case. About three months into the year I was poring through back issues of *Reader's Digest* and staring at Rand McNally maps of cities back home. Think culture shock affected me?

They taught me Chinese songs, puns, and phrases that made me sound more natural in Mandarin. My favorite: "Bu chi bai bu chi (*There's no point in not eating*)." I taught them English slang. Their favorite: "I'm freakin' out!"

Compared to their dorms my apartment was luxurious. They loved my kitchen (no cooking facilities in the dorms), bathtub (they paid to shower in a separate building), and combo washer/tumbler (a single appliance that dried clothes after washing them by spinning blindingly fast). Even my stained, unpadded carpet beat their bare concrete floors.

Those who were parents bragged about their offspring, one apiece. Henry joked that his son looked like an elephant. Chester boasted that his new-born daughter was "very beautiful and very fat." Historically the Chinese had preferred sons over daughters, so if the One Child Policy contributed anything positive to family dynamics (Chinese media referred to the rising generation, nearly all Only Children of two doting parents and four doting grandparents, as "little emperors"), it inspired parents to cherish their little girls. My students who had daughters bragged about them with abandon.

Toward the end of the evening they'd corral themselves by calling out "Zou ba (*Let's go*)," and would depart as they arrived, as a whole group. *Goodbye* was "Zai jian" – simple enough, except that a novice like me was prone to reverse the phrase, to great comedic effect. "Jian zai" meant *I'm still alive.* Thus I occasionally bid farewell to my Free Talk guests by declaring my con-

Meat vendor

tinued existence. It drew fits of laughter every time.

. . .

WHAT'D YOU THINK of real Chinese food?" people asked when I returned to America.

"I don't know," I replied, "I never had any." Not technically true, but it did express a truth: I ate the majority of my meals with students in the canteen, and they disavowed the food as anything resembling Chinese.

For breakfast I bought staples from Wudaokou: bananas, peaches, oatmeal, eggs and PBJ. The same brands of peanut butter and jam changed recipe from jar to jar, contributing a degree of variety to my otherwise monotonous diet. I particularly enjoyed the grapes – close to ping-pong size, with skin so thick it needed to be peeled.

In the winter I frequented the teacher canteen for its higher quality meals drenched in oil. With the climate so dry, and radiator heat even drier, my face perpetually flaked unless I ate the oily noodles. You do what works.

By May, no longer able to stand the student canteen, I got hooked on takeout from a nearby Korean shack erected around a tree growing through the tin roof. (If you've never tasted bi bim bop, a meat and vegetable stir fry with rice, trust me – stop by your local Korean restaurant and give it a try.)

So basically the only authentic Chinese food I ate was during that first week of random menu pointing, and then about once a month when students invited me out to a restaurant. By that count, some Americans eat Chinese more often than I did in actual China.

I can verify that there weren't fortune cookies. When I described them to my students, they accused me of fibbing.

I was surprised to see that they didn't mix their entrées with rice. They saved the rice for last – it brushed the teeth, cleansed the palette and left a subtly sweet aftertaste. A year in Beijing gave me the ability to distinguish good rice from bad; to this day I'm astounded by the many "good" Chinese restaurants in America that serve lousy rice.

Returning to the original question, then. The few times I ate authentic Chinese food, I enjoyed it. Oilier than I expected; in Beijing, a little bland; dishes often included vegetables I've never seen in America.

And yes, it beat our Chinese take-out.

. . .

DA SHI TANG was for me a trial-by-fire experience. Don't worry, I won't leave you in a similar predicament. Should you ever find yourself in a Chinese student canteen, consult this handy guide so you too can navigate your way to a lukewarm meal.

Seating approximately three hundred in a room that doubled as an auditorium, tripled as a dance floor, quadrupled as a movie theater and quintupled as an indoor badminton court, Da Shi Tang served breakfast, lunch and dinner.

PREPARATION

1. Buy a Meal Ticket Purchasing Card from somewhere. Your waiban will tell you this is a difficult process; indeed, he's not really sure how it's done. But he knows that each student is allowed only one card, and this rule is very strict. Eventually you'll discover the Photocopy Lady keeps these cards in an old recipe box, charges five mao each, and is willing to sell you ten or twenty if you're so inclined. Your Meal Ticket Purchasing Card is about twice the size of a business card, white with green print. Heed the directions:

此证妥为保存，用完后以旧换新，遗失罚款。
不准转借，涂改作废，离校交回。
盖章有效。

2. Purchase meal tickets from the Da Shi Tang office. They're sold in groups of three yuan and are color-coded by value, which is printed in Chinese characters. Review these numbers for easy recall:

一 二 三 四 五 六 七 八 九 十

3. Purchase a rice bowl from a local store (six yuan). Included is a plate that fits over the bowl to retain heat; both are made of iron covered with a ceramic layer that will begin chipping away soon. Also buy a spoon (five

*Crepe meal tickets
bought as a packet
secured by one staple*

*Sign of progress – paper tickets
were replaced by plastic*

mao). Don't worry about impressing anyone with your chopstick ability – in the canteen students eat with spoons and will consider you strange for not doing so.

4. Meal times are 5:30PM for dinner, 11:30AM for lunch, and too early for breakfast. Da Shi Tang fills up ten minutes before each of these times. Bring bowl, plate, spoon, and one packet of meal tickets. The bowl and plate will fit snugly in the spring-action carry rack on your bicycle until the spring breaks, at which point you will ride one-handed, carrying your bowl. Give others along the way a cheery "Ni chi le ma (*Have you eaten?*)" – a greeting of implied concern for their well-being, equivalent to America's "How are you?"

ACQUISITION

5. Hot dishes sell out quickly, so start here. They're sold from the windows opposite the entrance, behind the swarm of bodies. No dallying! A warm meal depends on your technique within this shoving, steaming, in-your-ear-breathing mass of hunger. Suggested position: one arm low with your bowl at the waist, the other hand on the shoulder ahead. Keep your torso sideways and lean forward on the balls of your feet. Gains and losses occur when someone leaves the windows and the crowd shifts – a misalignment of shoulders or feet could cost you minutes. Be especially wary of women who exploit their smaller builds to slip under armpits. When you near the windows, thrust your bowl forward between the heads of those in front of you.

(If you wait politely for your "turn," you will obtain only a big serving of frustration. Don't expect others to abide by your ways. They're not in your country – you're in theirs.)

6. Meals and prices are listed in Chinese characters on the chalkboard above the windows. Entrées are prepared in gigantic steel bowls, but due to poor line of sight and the dinginess of the glass you may not be able to identify the offerings. Don't worry: if you indicate the wrong meal, the server will slop your mistake back into its bowl and grant you a second try.

7. Servers can't hear much over the din, nor can they see your face through the glass, so point out your choice. If it's close, say "zhe ge (*this*)"; if far, "na ge (*that*)." When he reaches for your bowl among the half-dozen others shoved through the window and requests confirmation, affirmation is "dui," negation "bu" – or, more commonly, a string of bu's: "bubububu, na ge," then point again. Ask the price using your trusty phrase "Zhe ge duo shao qian?" By this point your verbal ineptitude will tip him off to the fact that your hand belongs to one of the foreign teachers, prompting him to announce with comical exaggeration: "LIU MAO (*SIX DIMES*)!" Hand over

your meal tickets. Although he accepts tickets from others without counting, he will verify yours.

8. Food obtained, extricate yourself from the tangle of arms and pressing bodies. A rear-first scoot works best.

9. Repeat steps 5-8 at other windows to acquire rice, steamed bread and/or other sides.

SEATING

10. Tables are small, circular, designed for four but typically seat eight. A few groups of students will beckon. Choose carefully: you don't want to favor some students over others through unequal attention.

11. Find a stool. Da Shi Tang has enough for about three at each table. Your students will offer theirs; when you decline they'll help you acquire one. To ask if a stool is reserved: "You mei you ren (*Have or have not a person*)?" Listen intently, as the two answers, "You (*Have*)" and "Mei you (*Have not*)," sound alike, and a muttered response in all the noise is easily mistaken. Be nimble – no stool remains unoccupied long, and brief scuffles occur.

CONVERSATION

12. Students *eat* in the canteen; they *talk* anywhere else. But they'll want to spend time with you, so they'll compromise by conversing through full mouths. Understanding low-vocab English in a Chinese accent through a mouthful of rice in a noisy canteen is a skill you will master within weeks.

13. Discussion topics range from cultural differences to personal histories to English slang ("No way," "Gag me," and "What a spazz"). Language gaffes abound, such as "That was a great orgy we had last night" (the danger

At Da Shi Tang
with students

of a thesaurus). You may hear playful complaints about workload: "I have bought this big bowl because you are giving so much homework, I need to eat more." A favorite game is Teach Lao Wai to Speak Mandarin. Despite laughter at your attempts, students will appreciate your efforts and provide appropriate coaching, such as "Open your mouse (*mouth*)."

14. As the table guest you will speak most, invariably making you last to finish eating. Your students will enjoy your company, but they'll still consider Da Shi Tang no place for talking. Consequently they will twitch, gazing at other tables long vacated – yet they must remain with you or lose face. Continue eating. Skirt any awkwardness with self-deprecatory statements such as "Wo chi tai man le (*I eat too slowly*)" – otherwise you'll find yourself losing too much weight.

EXEUNT

15. Upon finishing announce "Zou ba!" Everyone will head for the sinks near the entrance. Dump excess food into the overflowing bins, then rinse your bowl. Many students fill their bowls from the taps to drink. Don't do this. And when you get home, be sure to scrub your bowl with soap.

. . .

XIA HAI, the term for private enterprise, expressed more than a little Communist apprehension. Literally it meant "fall into the sea."

By 1993 the Communist Party had crafted reforms that allowed average people to start their own businesses. Strictly speaking, the nation had strayed beyond Communism to become a "socialist market economy with Chinese

Vegetable seller

characteristics." Suddenly anyone could sell goods and pocket the profits.

Not all were eager to fall into the sea of business, but many tried. At Wudaokou people rented stalls to sell vegetables, fruit, beans, rice, eggs, beef, fish, chicken – anything that could be bought from surrounding farms. (I once watched a chicken slaughter. Right there in the market a man pulled a chicken from a cramped wire pen, scissor-snipped a hole in its neck, and dropped it into a covered basket to flap and bleed itself to death.)

The xia hai convenience store near my apartment was actually the front room of a family hutong. Here I bought snacks for Free Talks, plus toilet paper, bottled water, Coke, and a delicious yogurt-type drink. Many types of products I didn't recognize, and although I could ask "Zhe shi shen me (*What is this*)," I usually failed to comprehend the answers. The shopkeeper, a chipper woman named Hua Dongmei, tallied each bill on an abacus. She was pleasantly plump – a sign that business was good.

At subway stations, candied cherry vendors lined up side by side and watched, owl-eyed, the people passing by. Each stand was identical to every other. Beneath a political machine that stressed the value of conformity, many who ventured into business did so as Communists, following their peers and leaving customer choice up to a Plinko-like fate. I'm no businessman, but growing up in America I couldn't help but absorb some baseline salesmanship. I wanted to pick one random man out of the candied cherry row and say, "Come on, get aggressive! Move to another spot, make a sign, offer extras and a family discount. And for Pete's sake, smile!"

To be fair, I had limited exposure to Beijing's true economic pulse. North of all three ring roads, Lin Da was well removed from the business movers and shakers. *China Daily* regularly heralded new joint ventures with foreign

"*Gan bei* (cheers)!"
*A classy outing with Beijing
sophisticates*

corporations. Some of my own students were riding this wave of better-paying jobs in sales and marketing. Corporate ladders were rising, and they relished the opportunity to climb.

A small group of these students invited me out for dinner and a concert downtown. Picture me (22, unmarried, lacking in style, somewhat clueless even in my own country) with them: late twenties to mid thirties, married, established, sharply dressed, members of the more sophisticated Beijing of fine restaurants and cultured entertainment. Looking back, their inclusion of a foreign kid with shabby clothes and overgrown hair demonstrated the finest level of class: taste mixed with grace.

. . .

> *DEAR FRIENDS: We are all Mr. Hobson's students. He teaches us only more than a month, but we have deep feelings now. We loved him. And from him we know you. Now many of us want to write to you. The follows are what we want to say.*
>
> *Grace: Hello, I'm glad to write to you. I hope we can become good friends.*
>
> *Leon: I'm a student and very glad to write to you. My home is in Hangzhou. He has a very beautiful lake – West Lake. If you have a chance to come to China, you're welcome to Hangzhou.*
>
> *Besides these, another students want to ask you several questions.*
>
> *Emily: What do the students like best to do in America? How do they spend their spare time.*
>
> *Sarah: If every American is proud of his country?*
>
> *Henry: Could you tell me about the tourism of America such as the beautiful place, antique and the cost used for tourism every year.*
>
> *And I'm Hannah: I want to say, I'm glad to write to you and love you, too. Welcome to China. Give you my best wishes!*
>
> *Yours sincerely,*
>
> *The students in Class P3*

. . .

A FULL-COURSE UNIVERSITY BANQUET? I saved my appetite all day.

Which was ironic, as I left the banquet hungrier than when I arrived.

This proved to be a rule: the more formal the occasion, the more cinematic the food. Jellyfish. Fermented tofu. Cow stomach. At each banquet I took the obligatory nibbles, smiled, and wondered why they couldn't serve something simple like noodles. I did enjoy a few offerings, such as black rice deluged in sugary paste, bamboo shoots boiled to broccoli tenderness, and zesty, jerky-style beef strips.

Thousand year eggs disturbed me. "They're not really buried for a thousand years," I said.

"No no no," the department chair reassured. "More like one hundred days." The jellified result was an egg white turned translucent charcoal, with the yolk forest green. Surprisingly neutral in taste, it coated my mouth with a fine, Oxy 10-ish film that persisted the rest of the evening, no matter what I ate or drank afterward.

Aside from sport eating, banquets provided a stage for local entertainment – *very* local, performed by attendees themselves. After the meal and speeches and toasts, people took turns standing and singing in a kind of karaoke, minus the screen and lights. Voices cracked, faces beamed and words were forgotten, drawing laughter and called-out reminders. Not everyone volunteered to sing, but it was expected that each subgroup or department would participate. I joined the five other foreign teachers at Lin Da in exhibiting a bit of Americana: "The Star-Spangled Banner," "O Susanna" and "Gilligan's Island."

Occasionally others played instruments or recited poetry. After two banquets I decided I'd had it with the cheesy American songs and prepared a different act: devil sticks. You may have seen devil sticks – two batons used to strike a larger, counterbalanced stick, causing it to tilt and spin in midair (some pros light the middle one on fire). After picking up a few tricks from my brother I'd brought a set to Beijing, and practiced with fury once I'd decided to embarrass myself with them.

The next banquet, hosted by the president of my organization in conjunc-

*University
banquet*

tion with government officials, took place in downtown Beijing. It was the fanciest (read: most unappetizing) spread I'd seen, with more than a hundred people in attendance, including a seventy-year-old Communist Party senator attended by a bodyguard. The stakes were high, the pressure on. Suppose no one performed quirky acts at banquets – would I be considered rude?

Wielding sticks like nunchakus flashing in the air, I stood not ten feet from the senator's seat beside the performance area. Her bodyguard glared at me the whole time. I fought away visions of losing control and crashing the weighted stick into the elderly senator's face, causing a heart attack and death, whereupon I would be arrested, convicted as a CIA operative and locked away in one of those horrible Chinese prisons my mother had warned me would kill her if I ended up in.

Miraculously I didn't flub once, not even on the high spinning toss. And miraculously, everyone applauded – the most appreciation coming, of course, from my American colleagues. My performance meant they didn't have to sing.

. . .

OUR FOREIGN LANGUAGE DEPARTMENT was going to plant trees in the Gobi Desert, and I was invited.

Without much in the way of grubbies, I donned jeans and a t-shirt, only to board the bus and find no one else dressed casually. Oh well, let them dirty their nice clothes.

Year by year the Gobi encroached on Beijing, causing dust storms and blighting usable land. Trees prevented erosion and held the desert back. The cause itself didn't mean much to me, but since I was new to Beijing, teaching at a forestry university that coordinated projects like this one, I appreciated being included. Besides, who doesn't like trees? On the two hours out I added this experience to the list of Things to Tell My Future Grandchildren: dear old gramps fought the voracious Gobi Desert. A genuine Johnny Appleseed, me.

At a gate in the middle of desolation we picked up a guide who directed our bus to a hillside of terraced dirt. I'd envisioned crowds working feverishly, backhoes digging, trucks hauling in a forest of saplings, but the area was perfectly still. No noise, not even a breeze. Just crusty dirt.

A few rows of trees were already planted. Along one terrace we noticed a dozen bagged saplings and some shovels. Our guide gestured to the shovels.

In minutes I finished my first planting, brushed my hands and looked around. "Where are the other trees?"

"Good job," the department chair said. "That is all."

"Aren't there more trees to plant?"

"More?" He looked confused. "The workers will plant more."

Workers? I scanned the wasteland around us. No one.

One by one my colleagues finished, wiped their hands, clapped each other on the back. We boarded the bus.

So much for my brave battle against the desert. Somewhere on a dry hillside two hours out from Beijing, I dug a hole, plopped a sapling in it, and covered it with dirt. I'd expected a sweaty workday; I participated instead in a ceremonial gesture.

On the way home we celebrated our work at an extravagant restaurant.

For which I was shamefully underdressed.

. . .

THEY ALL KNEW JOHN DENVER'S "COUNTRY ROADS." A Mandarin cover must have played throughout China. Now my students wanted to learn it in English, probably so they could impress their friends in karaoke.

I'd taught them a few English songs already, but this one they wanted to belt with gusto – a wee disruptive in a hall of cinder block classrooms with no carpeting and high ceilings. Since they weren't strong on the verses or the fast-worded bridge ("I hear her voice, in the morning hours she calls me ..."), I kept them hushed by directing them back to those lines: "Wait, we've got to practice that bridge again, we still didn't get it right ..."

Fighting the Gobi

Only at the end of class did I let them at the refrain. Students from nearby rooms crowded our door to watch us crooning our undying loyalty to the hills of West Virginia.

Why "Country Roads"? I doubted it was just the catchy tune. The Chinese must have connected with the song's theme: "Take me home to the place where I belong." Home was a serious value in China, even more than in America. Nearly every person I met told me their hometown, even if it was a backwater. "My city makes excellent vinegar," Heather said of Taiyuan. "Perhaps you have eaten it. It is excellent."

"Yes, yes," her classmates affirmed, "it is excellent vinegar. You must taste it."

Vinegar. What a peculiar claim to fame. Yet Heather was adamant, to the point of bringing me a bottle after a weekend trip home. I tried it on my jiaozi (*dumplings filled with meat or veggies*), and yup: it was vinegar. Evidently my waiguoren taste buds lacked the proper connoisseurship.

Often studying far from home, college students pressed the rail lines when holidays approached. The few of mine who couldn't make it home pitched themselves headlong into endearing cases of doldrums.

In late September families gathered for the Moon Festival, a sort of Thanksgiving with a feast and tasty little moon cakes stuffed with nuts and dry fruit. The students I found moping in Da Shi Tang that weekend taught me a Moon Festival poem. No doubt it lost a degree of eloquence in its translation over bowls of rice. Still, as I wrapped up my first full month in Beijing, this poem reminded me how far I was from America, and how long an entire year could be.

The moonlight comes in through the window
and touches the foot of my bed.
Lift up your head,
*   look at the moon.*
Lower your head,
*   look at the shadow of the moon,*
*   and think about home.*

Kunming Lake at Yihe Yuan :: Qianmen Gate at Tiananmen

FALL

In every apartment building I visited a distinct fragrance saturated the air. Thanks to tight quarters and thin walls, hallways drummed in the afternoons with the rhythm of knives on cutting boards – women chopping ingredients for that night's stir fry. I came to anticipate the aroma of soy sauce whenever I walked through a lobby.

That made me wonder: if I associated their homes with the smell of soy sauce, what smell did they associate with Americans?

None, right? Americans were neutral-smelling. Weren't we?

It was worth asking. "You know," I said during Free Talk, "apartments in Beijing all smell like soy sauce to me."

"Really?" Their fascination told me I was on to something.

I continued, "What do you think Americans smell like?"

They didn't even pause: "Milk!"

Milk?

It made sense: the Chinese rarely drank milk or used it in their cooking (many were lactose intolerant), whereas Americans consume it constantly: baking, breakfast cereal, cheese, yogurt, ice cream, coffee creamer. We practically bathe in it. Any wonder, then, milk exudes from our pores in a vanilla-esque way we don't notice?

Yet my students had never been to America. How did they form this impression? Was it a stereotype, akin to Rosie O'Donnell's "Ching chong, ching ching chong" impression of their language? (Incidentally, I loved their mock English: guttural, choppy syllables of nonsense, mostly B's, G's and D's, highlighting English's Germanic roots. Tuck your chin and quack out a staccato version of babytalk for the idea.) Did Chinese citizens who'd traveled to America return home with reports of milk odors?

Their impression couldn't have been based on me. I was just one person, eating the same food they ate.

Except …

During my first weeks in Beijing, the instant dairy-free diet stunned me. My body craved milk. My mother, worried about the impending drop in my calcium intake, had packed me a box of dairy supplements, chalky tablets the consistency of Pepto Bismol pills that tasted uncannily like milk. Within weeks I was scarfing four or five tablets a day. Who knew dairy withdrawal was possible?

By the time the tablets ran out I'd discovered a local dairy source: naifen (*powdered milk*), sold at government grocery stores in foil packets of various flavors, including soy, black bean, and goat. My favorite was powdered yak milk, a creamy sweet Tibetan specialty. Each day I drank several glasses, mixing the powder with less and less water until eventually I was spooning straight from the packet.

No wonder they thought Americans smelled like milk. I must've reeked!

. . .

WHAT DOES THIS MEAN? I saw it in a movie."

I looked up. Henry was flipping me the bird.

He looked at me quizzically, his middle finger proud. It was really up there. Some people couch theirs between bent index and ring knuckles, but his was the defiant fist-and-finger version.

My apartment kitchen

"No, don't," I winced, waving him off. "That's ... very bad. Don't do that."

The others scrutinized Henry's gesture. "What is so bad? What does it mean?" Their fingers fumbled until they got it. Sixteen students were flicking me off.

"Don't say this," I warned, "this is very bad." On the whiteboard I spelled the epithet. Of course they said it anyway, working carefully at the pronunciation. "Yes, we are always hearing this in the movies."

"Please don't say it, ever. It's the worst thing you can say in English."

That *really* got their attention. "What does it mean?"

I sighed. "Well, the first word means *sex*."

They giggled. "That sounds like it would be good," Rick ventured.

I grimaced. "No, it's not. It's bad sex." From their expressions I could tell I wasn't making sense.

Henry saved me. He'd finally ascertained The Finger's biological symbolism and whispered something in Mandarin, making everyone laugh. Then Martha said something else in Mandarin, and a few gasped. Middle fingers dropped; chuckles subsided, replaced by blushes.

Whatever Martha said would suffice. "Okay, back to our lesson ..."

. . .

COMPOSITION: EXPLAIN A MISTAKE YOU WILL NEVER FORGET.

> *When I was five years old, I always thought I knew everything in the world. One day I went to my neighborhood, a little girl's home. Her parents bought a small basket of jasmine bud. But because of the dull weather, the jasmine wasn't flower but bud. They seemed to be very*

With students at Beihai Park

*disappointed at this because they couldn't make them into jasmine tea.
I asked my friend why we couldn't make the jasmine bud blossom. She
also thought so. What should we do? Suddenly I had an idea. When the
sun shines on the bud, it will blossom. It must be the heat that makes
it do. Such being the case, we could heat the bud by vapor and make
them blossom. (You can imagine how stupid the idea is.) After about
thirty minutes passed, there was only cooked bud full of water. Suddenly
my pal cried and said her parents might spank her. I was very worried.*

*Now whenever I think of this thing, I feel it is the stupidest and
most ridiculest thing. It is the thing that makes me know there are many,
many things I don't know in the world. The world is infinite. No one
can know the world clearly. Only to study is to know more.*

. . .

WHAT A PREPOSTEROUS STEREOTYPE, that they all looked alike! I spent a year
among one billion Chinese citizens, and every individual looked wholly unlike every other.

True, skin tone, hair color, even stature and weight fell within a tighter
range compared to America's mixed salad of ethnicities. But that didn't make
everyone resemble everyone else. Far from it.

"Mistah Hobison," my students complimented, "your hair is so dark!"

"What are you talking about?" I asked, perplexed. "My hair's brown –
yours is black."

"No, *my* hair is brown. My hair is more brown than yours I think."
They distinguished finer degrees of hair color, which made sense: no hair is
truly black, only darker shades of brown. Apparently mine appeared darker
than some of theirs, which amused them – Americans were supposed to be
Baywatch-blond.

I couldn't tell a Roman nose from Greek, Nubian or any other type, but
they seemed to describe noses, chins, skin tone with precision. They even
described walking styles. "He has a great walk," they'd comment, "how to say
in English …" They'd trail off in words, then simply imitate the walk, with
everyone smiling, "Yes, yes!"

Intrigued, I asked about my walk. Rick thought a moment, then strode
across the room. It didn't look distinctive to me, just walking, but my students applauded. "Yes, you have a good walk," they said, which made me
self-conscious. What else were they noticing about me?

Over months of squeezing on buses and riding in thick bicycle traffic, I
played a mental game: could I spot *anyone* who looked like any other Chinese

person I knew? Consistently I failed – a testimony to the stunning uniqueness of the human face.

Evidently the game didn't work the other way. During the first week of class, my students had trouble distinguishing me from my teammate. We were both slender, thin-faced, with glasses and dark hair; that Jeff stood four inches above me didn't quite register. "It was very strange at first," they later confessed. "You walked out of the classroom and came back, and we wondered how you got so tall!"

. . .

WE LEARNED QUICKLY, we Americans, never to leave our apartments without first pocketing a wad of toilet paper. Public restrooms didn't provide it.

How much one carried was a personal calculation based on how long one planned to be out, how frequently one had to, ahem, *go*, and how sanitary one liked to be.

A side benefit of carrying your own toilet paper: no disappointment over restroom offerings. If one preferred cushy triple-ply, one could be pleased to use it everywhere.

I opted for the cheap stuff made from recycled paper products, with colors and print scraps (some large enough to read) flecking the cardboard-brown tissue. It was as ridged as crepe paper, three times stiffer ... and if that sounds unsavory, it's only because you've never used it. One wipe and you were *clean*.

Stores sold softer, more expensive brands, but why mess with perfection?

. . .

UP FOR A LANGUAGE PUZZLE?

ME: How do you say "How do you say this in Mandarin" in Mandarin?
STUDENT: Yes, what do you want to say?

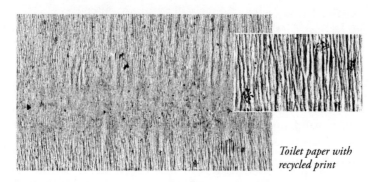

Toilet paper with
recycled print

M: "How do you say this in Mandarin?"

S: What is it?

M: That's it. In Mandarin I want to be able to ask, "How do you say this in Mandarin?"

S: Yes, please tell me what you want to say.

M: The question! I want to be able to use Mandarin to ask the question, "How do you say this in Mandarin?"

S: I am sorry, I am not understanding you.

Eventually I gave up.

. . .

MISTAH HOBISON, how do you think about Taiwan?"

After a colonial period of over 150 years, Great Britain was preparing to return Hong Kong to China. The transfer was certain, etched in stone – and only four years away. My students anticipated the event with excitement, along with a sense of inevitability that spilled into their thoughts about Taiwan.

Of course regular political lessons on the necessity of Taiwan's return, whether through diplomacy or military force, helped to keep the island at the forefront of their minds.

When Mao Zedong led the Communist Revolution, the prior government fled to Taiwan, where they continued governing an area not even one percent the size of the mainland. Why should China obsess over such a small renegade? I suspected Communists had trouble stomaching Taiwan's economic success in the face of their own struggles.

That I voiced no opinion about Taiwan was, in the minds of my students, opinion enough. My tactful evasions turned their tones serious:

"Taiwan belongs to China."

"Taiwan must come back."

"We await the day when Taiwan will return to our country."

And they'd shake their heads and add, "Perhaps the army will be needed."

. . .

EARLY EACH MORNING members of the Lin Da work unit, young, old and retired, filed out to the campus track to walk or jog. This habit seemed more cultural than mandatory. At one end groups practiced tai chi, the slow, meditative martial arts form.

"Should I learn tai chi?" I asked my students.

They giggled. "No no no no no, tai chi is for girls!"

"What?" I hadn't realized that the groups I'd seen were all-female.

"Yes, tai chi is too slow for boys."

"Then what do boys do for exercise?"

"Basketball!"

. . .

THEY LOVED AMERICA. They hated America. I wondered if the whole nation was schizophrenic.

Each morning in *China Daily*, top-level Communists denounced the evils of American influence, American human rights abuses, American support for Taiwan, and overall Americanism. One might believe the world consisted of only two nations, China and America, the incessant infractions of one eliciting ever-faithful rebukes from the other.

Simultaneously other *China Daily* articles celebrated joint ventures between American and Chinese corporations. They seemed to focus on economics even more than Americans do, yearning to come alongside us as business partners.

The only newspaper in English, *China Daily* toed the party line so closely I felt I was eavesdropping on what the Chinese read in their own papers. At subway stations, vendors hawked fifteen or twenty news publications in different sizes and colors – a surprising variety of coverage.

"Which newspaper is the best?" I asked students.

"What do you mean?"

"Which newspaper do you trust the most? Which one do you read?"

They waved off the question: "No no no, they are all the same."

"The same? There's more than a dozen newspapers."

"Yes, the stories are the same. Even the pictures are the same."

So much for journalistic freedom. Multiple publications all saying the same thing must have been the Communist means of multiplying job opportunities.

I read *China Daily* religiously, in part for the stream of contemporary English, in part for the intellectual exercise of guessing at larger world events through its ideological screen. I was especially vigilant for one headline: "Deng Xiaoping Dead." Word had it his health had deteriorated, and my teaching organization had warned that if this occurred, pro-democracy demonstrations might flare up again, incurring another crackdown. Only four years earlier the Tiananmen event had prompted Americans to evacuate.

Mao Zedong's immediate successor, Deng Xiaoping, rarely appeared in public that year, yet his political works made huge headlines, along with calls for Party members to "unify their thinking, solidify their political belief, resolutely implement the Party's basic line." This sounded to me like a buildup to a transition. Secretly I hoped to witness so historic an event as Deng's passing. Communist leaders were long-lived; from the 1949 revolution to that year, China had had only two.

Paucity of news about the actual man convinced some of us that Deng had *already* died, and was being kept under wraps while the Communist Party resolved internal power struggles. We based this speculation on the evident one-upmanship of the two leaders beneath Deng: President Jiang Zemin, a good ol' boy with deep Party connections; and Premier Li Peng, intellectual mastermind of the Three Gorges Dam project. They reminded me of Napoleon and Snowball from Orwell's *Animal Farm*. If Li Peng had read that book, its warnings escaped him, for when Deng finally died (three years after I left), Jiang Zemin had little difficulty consolidating power and relegating his adversary to obscurity.

I made my own appearance in a Chinese newspaper when an undergrad interviewed me for Lin Da's student rag. During thirty minutes of questions she took zero notes – evidence of a superb memory, I assumed. Six weeks later, students surprised me with a battery of questions: "You didn't tell us you like gong fu (*kung fu*)! How long have you studied? Did you come to China to learn?"

The interview had been published, and somewhere in all those characters I was quoted as saying my interest in China began with gong fu movies. Had I said this? No – nor did I have any idea what gave her such an impression.

At least she included my plea to the Lin Da student body in a paragraph about my frequent appearances at Da Shi Tang: "Tell everyone to leave some of the best dishes for me!"

. . .

COMPOSITION: WHAT PERSONALITY TRAITS DO YOU ADMIRE?

> *I am an introvert, so I don't like to take part in collective activities. I have no one to talk with, to play with and just to look on nearby. Character can hardly be changed. Although I don't like my own character, I am used to the way in which I think and behave.*
>
> *When I am with an extrovert, I'll feel his fervor and that life is so colorful and hopeful. So sometimes how I want to be an extrovert. However, an extrovert sometimes will get into trouble with some insidi-*

ous and invidious persons. So my favorite character is disingenuousness. Because I am too honest and I'm afraid I will get into trouble when I go into the society. But it's very difficult to change the honesty.

AFTER THAT TROUBLESOME FIRST WEEK I honed my water boiling and cooling process. Before Free Talks I stocked my fridge with prepared water and offered it to students with pride.

One night they taught me a card game in which each round's loser performed a silly punishment, like spinning around ten times or singing a song. After one round someone suggested the loser should drink cold water.

"How is *that* punishment?" I asked.

It turned out that they believed cold water to be bad for the digestive system. They preferred hot water, evident in their regular consumption of tea (which also killed off microbes). To them, cold water down the esophagus felt equivalent to an ice cube sliding down one's back – great party mischief!

All that time I'd been serving them ice water.

. . .

WHY?" THEY PRESSED, stepping further into my personal space. "Why did Michael Jordan retire?"

"Did he?" Too busy to read *China Daily* that morning, I hadn't heard. Everyone else had, and they were grieving.

"He is best in the world."

"He should not retire."

"Please tell us why he retires."

"Look," I said, "I'm not in America, I'm here. You heard the news. Did they say why he retired?"

"No. Only that he is retired."

Perplexed, disturbed, they needed an answer – and found no comfort in me, who didn't really care. In this *they* were more American: many were devoted NBA fans, whereas I'd never watched a full game.

The rest of that year I heard over and over, when meeting new people: "Do you know Michael Jordan?" What a language trap!

Scenario A

Do you know Michael Jordan?

No.

You do not know Michael Jordan? Are you really from America?

69

(Laughter.) How can you not know Michael Jordan?

Scenario B
Do you know Michael Jordan?
Yes.
(Eyes widen in awe.) Really? You really know him?

Scenario C
Do you know Michael Jordan?
Not personally.
(Silence, wondering what "not personally" means.)

The only way out was a direct launch into the full explanation: "Yes, I know who Michael Jordan is, but I have never met him."

Of all things I expected from a year in China, regular specifications concerning my knowledge of Michael Jordan wasn't among them.

. . .

IT'S HARD ENOUGH convincing a new reader the word *sea* doesn't begin with the letter C. Imagine explaining to non-native speakers oddities like the GHs in *through* and *cough*.

English suckers us with false promises. Pronunciation should be as simple as decoding consonants and vowels; in reality, decoding causes errors. When my students stumbled over a word like *colonel* and I corrected them, I could see their eyes fill with exasperation. What a field of landmines – who knew where the next mispronunciation lurked?

Chinese characters were cut and dry. They posed no threat of mispronunciation because they didn't even pretend to offer phonetic information. A word like 北京 contained no clues about where to place lips or tongue, no hint at all about vocalization; the audible sounds of "Beijing" were tethered to the visible shapes 北京 only through memorization. So when the Chinese encountered characters they didn't recognize, they weren't able to guess their meaning by sounding them out. English speakers have a good shot at recognizing words unfamiliar in written form (like a baby's *onesie*), but Chinese speakers needed to consult a dictionary.

In a few cases, the components of a character gave clues. 木 meant *tree*; two 木 were used for *forest* 林; three 木 formed the word *wooded* 森. This made pictographic sense. But few characters were so pictographic, and even these three were pronounced differently ("mu," "lin," "sen").

Korean writing, by the way, is entirely different – Korean syllables are built by stacking consonant and vowel markers. A high school friend once gave me an impromptu lesson that in twenty minutes had me "reading" line after line of Korean, without a clue as to what I was saying. A quick phonetic primer would enable similar performances for languages like Greek or Russian, but not Chinese. Was it any surprise, then, that China's education system emphasized rote learning? Early years of tying audible sounds to visual symbols flavored later disciplines.

Compared to over ten thousand syllables in English, Mandarin used relatively few syllables – approximately four hundred, due mainly to the lack of final consonants (just N and NG). Fewer syllables resulted in more homonyms (words like our *tow* and *toe*) that provided greater opportunities for verbal puns but also required clarifications: "Is that Dear Abby's *dear*, or Bambi's *deer*?" I overheard such questions frequently in conversation.

Four hundred syllables really weren't enough for clear communication, so Mandarin differentiated using tones. *Ma*, for example, could be spoken in four ways: with a straight high tone ("mother"), a rising tone ("numb"), a low bouncing tone ("horse"), and a sharp falling tone ("scold"). These four tones practically quadrupled the tally of Mandarin sounds.

Newscasters spoke in beautiful, deliberate tones, yet everyday conversations were so rapid-fire I could hardly distinguish them. In fact I once accused my students of ignoring intonation altogether. They insisted the tones were in there, woven so tightly to pronunciation that garbling them would cause confusion. Imagine a new English speaker improperly stressing the syllables of a word like *photographer*: "PHO-to-GRAPH-er" just doesn't sound right. Even closer to Mandarin tonality would be a word *object*: "OB-ject" is entirely different from "ob-JECT."

. . .

CHINESE DICTIONARIES MYSTIFIED ME. How do you look up a drawing?

My students showed me that each character contained a root shape, or radical. The character *jing* 京 had the radical 亠, drawn by two brush or pen strokes. To find 京 in a dictionary, first scan the list of two-stroke radicals to find 亠, note its section of the dictionary and turn there, where common characters using 亠 were organized, in a Mandarin-English dictionary, by sound according to the English alphabet. (I supposed Mandarin-*Mandarin* dictionaries were organized by the Mandarin oral alphabet: *bo po mo fo de te ne le ge ke he ji qi xi zhi chi shi ri zi ci si*.)

Along with meaning, dictionaries gave pronunciation in the form of pinyin (literally "spell sound"), a Westernized phonetic system:

Characters: 我是美国人。
Pinyin: Wo shi Meiguoren.
English: I am an American.

Gradeschoolers learned pinyin as a set of training wheels before memorizing and writing actual characters.

Computers used pinyin for typing. For the sentence "Wo shi Meiguoren" they typed W-O, causing the screen to display a list of all characters corresponding to this syllable, the most common ("I") ranked first. Press 1 to select the proper character, then type the next word, S-H-I, and press the number for that character. This might seem cumbersome, but students said average typing speeds fell between forty and fifty words per minute. The most complex characters required just four or five keystrokes – comparatively short considering that even this sentence contains words of ten or more keystrokes.

Students described another keyboard, one that allowed still faster input. Used by professional typesetters, it contained over a hundred keys, each assigned a type of stroke. Users built a character stroke by stroke until the computer used process of elimination to determine the one intended. Mastering this system took a long time, but it allowed most words to be typed in two or three keystrokes, yielding typing speeds over a hundred characters per minute.

"Overly complicated," we English speakers think. "Give us the straight phonetics." To be sure, writing with blocks of sound has distinct advantages. Crossword puzzles, word finds and Scrabble fascinated my students with their near-mathematization of language. They reveled in the ability to read aloud long, complicated English passages without having any clue about content.

Yet English contains archaic spellings, history preserved in exceptions that befuddle even native speakers. Why three forms of *there/their/they're*? All are pronounced alike, and each is clear enough in context. We've already phoneticized some words (*catsup → ketchup, doughnut → donut*); why not streamline the rest? Sĕntĕnsĕz mīt lŏŏk līk this, hwĭch wŏŏd sēm ôfələ fŭnē ăt fûrst bŭt wŏŏd bēkŭm fŭmĭlyər ēnŭf ōvər tīm – prŏbəblē ōnlē ə mătûr ŭv wēks. A system like English Phonemic Representation would virtually dispel mispronunciation – no small victory considering that studies have linked dyslexia to languages with irregular spellings.

Of course a spelling revolution would never fly in America – we can't even adopt the metric system. Yet the Communist Party accomplished just such a linguistic overhaul. Chinese characters used to be quite elaborate – if you think 龙 is daunting, try the original version: 龍. Not every character changed, but many revisions were striking: 飞 replaced 飛, and 厅 replaced 廳. Declaring complex characters both cumbersome and elitist, the Communist Party simplified many to basic strokes, making literacy more achievable for everyone.

Such a transformation could succeed only through the forced coordination between publishers, businesses and schools made possible by strict autocracy (note that Taiwan, a capitalist democracy, still uses traditional characters). Still, credit the Communists for pulling it off, benefiting all Chinese language learners, national and waiguoren alike. As for fuddy-duddy wordsmiths, they could continue to appreciate traditional calligraphy to their hearts' content, perhaps even enjoying the increased esotericism.

The lack of phonetic information in Chinese characters did offer one tremendous advantage: different dialects could use the same writing system. Individuals from different regions unable to converse nevertheless could pass notes fluently – simplifying the efforts of both emperors and Communist leaders in maintaining control over such a linguistically diverse region.

. . .

COMPOSITION: MAKE A PHONE CALL TO ANY FAMOUS PERSON.

> *VOICE: Hello, Mr. Lincoln, how are you?*
>
> *LINCOLN: I'm very good, thank you. May I ask who's calling?*
>
> *V: Certainly. This is Mr. Ma from China. I want to know what about you recently.*
>
> *L: I'm very well in heaven. The God invited me and other famous people in history yesterday. We talked about man's world today. The God said, "Men are more greater than ever. They have invented so many kind things even I haven't thought of it." Then he took us to look at the scene of today's world. I looked at many changes have taken place from our alive years.*
>
> *V: Yes. There's many changes from your era. When you were the president of the US there were only 13 states but today there's fifty.*
>
> *L: OK, I've heard of it. But I can't look at it because of cloud.*
>
> *V: I think that it might made of dirt because of pollution.*
>
> *L: Pollution? I've never heard of it.*
>
> *V: There are 4 crisis in our era. They are population, energy, food and pollution.*

. . .

MAKING STUDENTS LAUGH was as easy as counting to ten – on my fingers.

They used fingers for counting too, but only on one hand. One was the thumb; two through five added a finger each. Then six through ten continued on the same hand, each resembling a letter from the sign language alphabet. If you take hands as place values, the highest number Americans can show on two hands is 55; the Chinese could flash a full 100 (tens in both places).

Students signed numbers too rapidly for me to follow, especially the last five. "Slow down!" I'd plead. "Do six again. Okay, and what was seven?" They'd sigh, show me again, and wonder how I could be so dense about something any four-year-old could rattle off.

"How do you do it in America?" they asked.

I held up my left hand and began: "One, two, three, four, five ..." When I raised my right and continued, "Six," the room erupted in laughter.

"What's so funny?"

"You need *two* hands to count to ten?"

"Sure."

"But what if you are holding something in the other hand?"

"I guess you set it down," I replied sheepishly. Our method looked pretty inefficient.

. . .

MISTAH HOBISON, did you hear about the Tiananmen Square?"

Four years after the massacre, the political climate still bristled. Our teaching organization had forbidden us from discussing Tiananmen Square with students, especially as several would be Party members.

Free Talks usually ranged from celebrities to cultural differences to whether I would marry a Chinese woman. Sometimes my students sang songs; often they bragged about their hometowns.

I'd been in Beijing just two months when they asked The Question. Had I heard about Tiananmen Square? They weren't seeking an official response, they wanted to know. They *needed* to know.

"Well, yes," I said, assuming as flat a tone as possible. "Most of the world heard about it. We watched it on TV."

They hushed and leaned in.

"Terrible," one said.

"Very, very sad," said another.

"There were many students."

"My friend was there," said Jerry. "She does not talk about it. She was there."

"It was very strange," said Grace. "Li Peng got on the television and he was yelling at the students to go home. His face was very red and he was yelling." She was amused. Chinese culture frowned on public displays of anger, a serious loss of face.

"There were –" Chester asked in Mandarin for a word, which someone supplied: "Tanks."

"Many students died."

Another laughed nervously. "The government said twelve students died. Only twelve. They died from, how to say …" With some pantomiming we came up with the word *trampling*. "The tanks came and the students ran and the students were trampling."

"No," interjected Wu Li Yan. "No one died. That is incorrect."

"But the Party says –"

"No," repeated Wu Li Yan. Usually bright and optimistic, he was in his early thirties, a card-carrying Party member with a polished grasp of English that matched his professional demeanor. In the videotape I sent home, Wu issued the most sincere invitation to my family and friends to visit China. Jokingly his classmates referred to him as Little Mao, a nickname I assumed came from political aspirations. There was no joking now as he repeated, "No one died in Tiananmen Square."

"If the government says twelve people died –" implored one classmate.

"No. You are incorrect. The government did not say anyone died. That is a lie from the students."

Everyone fell silent. Wu's eyes scrutinized those who had spoken, then bore down on me. The others, unwilling to look him in the eye, followed his lead and watched me.

"Maybe we should play Uno," I said.

Monument to the People's Heroes, rallying point in 1989

That was the only time I heard anyone mention the massacre.

. . .

EYES HOT, FINGERS TIGHTENING INTO MY ARM, the officer hollered in my face. Alternately he glared at my fellow teacher, similarly gripped by another officer.

We deserved it. We were at Mutianyu, a less visited section of the Great Wall. What you see in all the photos is Badaling, where great effort had gone into reversing the effects of erosion and vegetation. Mutianyu had been similarly restored, but at one end, raw wall tempted us with historicity. A sign across the barrier clearly forbade access. Itching for something genuine behind the official showmanship, my friend and I had climbed across anyway.

Here dirt and shrubs claimed the top surface. Side walls leered in toothy edges. We'd traveled past two crumbling watchtowers in amazement before a pair of huffing security guards caught up and seized us. Intent on what lay ahead, we hadn't even realized we were being pursued.

Yes, we were being brazen and immature. Yes, the officers were right to be furious. Curious or not, we'd behaved as though the rules didn't apply to us, and that warranted some measure of prosecution.

That concern made us retreat into meek submission. Our shoulders drooped, faces fell. "Dui bu qi (*I'm sorry*)," we kept repeating, "dui bu qi." This reaction had all the effect of a judo throw, using the attacker's momentum against him. Move *with* a push and the pusher topples.

Unrestored Great Wall at Mutianyu

So he did. After shouting for several minutes, the lead officer escorted us toward the main gate in silence. Then, as if possessed by a different personality, he began speaking in a lightened tone, agreeable, nearly jovial. He asked about our families; we asked about his. He allowed me to take a photo with his partner. By the time we reached the parking lot we were all great friends.

Bizarre? Welcome to *face*.

In a culture that valued harmony and conciliation, losing temper was shameful, a loss of face or respectability. Releasing his unbridled anger had made the officer supremely uncomfortable; our contrition had left him floundering out of context. The resulting snapback in his demeanor was so striking it was difficult to believe.

The need to save face disinclined the Chinese to say *no*. A flat negative shamed not only the issuer (selfish!), but also the receiver for making an inordinate request. Instead the Chinese hemmed and hawed – or even answered *yes* while intending not to deliver. Such responses (I called them "pocket vetoes") avoided embarrassing scenes of rejection. Lin Da's administrative staff used them often against me. The harshest instance occurred when I reserved the campus karaoke room for a party with students. I showed up with food, decorations, and nearly fifty students, only to be told the room was in use. The other side of the door was silent. I'd failed to realize I wasn't well enough connected to reserve the karaoke room, and had therefore maneuvered the clerk into a direct falsehood. We had to abandon our party.

During that year I grew into the habit of issuing pocket vetoes myself. It felt strangely comfortable to say *yes* but think inside, "In your dreams! You're asking too much of me." If by failing to deliver I left someone in the lurch, well, it was that person's fault for overstepping our relationship. Unfortunately I carried this habit back to America, where I lost a part-time job when I agreed to work on my day off and then failed to show.

Entailed in the pocket veto was the concept of *guanxi*, or relational "pull." In a nation that sought to distribute money evenly, people climbed in rank and prestige through favors granted to and obtained from others. It was all about connections. A stranger had zero guanxi, no connection to you whatsoever. If she was in need of a bicycle pump, or if she dropped her *dong xi* (*stuff*) all over the ground, you had no obligation to help, nor even any moral impetus, as doing so would obligate her to repay the favor. Newspapers sometimes ran letters about random acts of kindness (chasing down a fellow customer who'd left behind an expensive purchase; loaning a bicycle to a stranger about to miss a job interview because her bicycle was stolen) – an indication of their rarity.

Mental tabs kept relationships equitable: in helping me you could *expect* a returned favor. You could always try to release me from obligation with the phrase *mei you guanxi* ("doesn't have guanxi"); otherwise it would be incumbent upon you to allow me to reciprocate. Guanxi could be paid off with gifts, such as an artwork print or a music cassette. People even gave gifts preemptively. If I bought you something nice without occasion, you could expect that in a day or two I would ask you for an out-of-the-ordinary favor.

You could pay off what you owed one person by tapping into what someone else owed you. When my mother visited me in Beijing, the father of one of my students sent a cab to drive us to the Great Wall. "This must be expensive," I told Tony. "Tell your father thank you very much."

"No, it is nothing," Tony said. "My father helped this man, so he owes my father a favor." Tony was connected to his father, who was connected to the driver of our cab, who therefore drove waiguoren he didn't know to the Great Wall.

You may wonder how I paid off such a huge favor. It wasn't the only one – my students showered Mom with gifts. Every time she unwrapped an ornate tea cup or calligraphy scroll, I winced. "Keep enjoying it," I whispered. "You get to hop on a plane and leave. I'll be stuck paying off all this guanxi." What would my students expect in return?

Thankfully, nothing. After waiting several weeks for the other shoe to drop, I finally asked a class leader, who assured me they'd acted out of simple hospitality. Besides, the notoriously low salaries of Chinese teachers instilled in students a sense of obligation. Mine had used Mom's visit to balance it out.

Beyond the classroom I was fairly guanxiless. I knew practically no one beyond Lin Da's Foreign Language Department. I couldn't offer anyone free meals or hotel stays or car access or anything of the sort. My only asset was English. Occasionally strangers approached me to ask for tutoring, and I could have cultivated these opportunities to develop my guanxi. But whenever I was away from students I wanted to learn Mandarin, so I declined all requests and consequently remained a featherweight.

Guanxi operates in America, too, just more subtly. I can't imagine anyone here giving me a framed painting in order to ask for tutoring.

. . .

No dogs. That was law.

Market reforms were enabling some individuals to cash in, pull ahead of the pack, and enjoy a few luxuries, like pets. But in a system that still valued corporate over individual achievement, and with rural conditions lagging sorely behind those of cities, shoveling superfluous wealth into a nonhuman mouth struck many as wrong.

One morning *China Daily* publicized a new police assignment: four officers tasked with solving dogs. Armed with nightsticks, they'd already encountered and beaten to death two pets in front of their horrified owners. Patrols would continue.

Discussing this initiative during Free Talk, students mentioned that Beijing once had tried to exterminate all sparrows. The government set poisoned food on rooftops across the city and the sparrows disappeared – to the great delight of the insects. They exploded in numbers, their populations unchecked. The poison was removed, and the sparrows gradually returned.

At least the anti-dog initiative was restrained. Four officers in a city of ten million was a mere gesture.

My own feelings were mixed. Wanton destruction of life unnerved me, but there was something compelling about a moral system that objected to pets as long as human mouths went empty.

. . .

IN 2006 I CHUCKLED at a BBC headline: "Beijing Clamps Down on Spitting."

Not everyone spat. Most of my students considered it gross, embarrassing. Still, the habit was pervasive enough that the wise watched their footsteps. One afternoon I just missed the line of fire when a fellow teacher got initiated (in the coat, thankfully, not the face) by a man aiming negligently out the window of a passing cab.

The problem wasn't only saliva: on sidewalks I occasionally saw adults finger-clamp one nostril, then expel the contents of the other.

You've probably heard of split pants. Instead of diapers, toddlers wore pants open from crotch to rear, baring their tenderest flesh to the world. I was fortunate never to have witnessed this feature's eliminatory use.

Even more discomforting for me were the spit trays on cafeteria and restaurant tables. The Chinese tended to serve meats in a "chainsaw chicken" manner, using vertical cleaver cuts to transform animals into geometric cubes. The resulting cross-sections, though biologically fascinating, made for less effective consumption when dining without fork or knife.

Enter the spit tray. Insert meat cube into mouth, grind, separate savory parts from indigestible. Swallow the former, then open wide and let gravity draw the latter into the rectangular tray at table center.

In the absence of a spit tray, the plastic tablecloth served as an acceptable point of oral deposit.

. . .

Has anyone seen Qian?"

Eyes averted.

"Is he sick?" I asked. Qian Da Liang was absent for the third day in a row.

"Yes, he is sick," answered Esther, one of his close friends. "Very sick." Heads nodded.

"Is he okay? Does he need a doctor?"

"No no no, he is okay, but he is very sick."

That afternoon I bicycled to the men's dorm. Students waiting for the lobby phone directed me to the right room. I didn't know what help I could offer – did Lin Da have a clinic? – but I figured I could find out. Like me, Qian was away from home, and I knew if I was sick enough to miss three straight days of class I would appreciate some concern.

The instant Qian saw me his face blanched. "Oh! I am so sorry, so sorry!" he gushed.

"No, you're not in trouble," I said. "I just want to make sure you're okay."

"Oh, yes." He smiled with embarrassment. "Please come in."

I hesitated – just how sick was he? Given his eager hospitality, however, I was unsure about the etiquette for declining, so I stepped inside.

The room looked considerably bare. A banker's lamp on the single desk illuminated a jumble of open books. Discarded peanut shells littered the concrete floor (standard practice was to sweep up at the end of the day). More books were strewn about the tousled bed. A room this size typically housed three students, but I noted only one other bed, and it lacked sheets. "You

Boy wearing split pants in Xiahe, western China

don't have roommates?" I asked.

"Roommates? Oh. The university needed the furniture. For other rooms."

That sounded strange, but I let it pass. "You look pretty well. You must be getting better."

He seemed confused.

"It must be hard being sick away from home."

"Sick? But I am not. Ah," his face lit. "The class said this."

"So you're not sick."

"No, I am sorry."

"Then ...?"

Here Qian began an extended tap dance as to why he was skipping class. He was registered to take the GRE in the spring, and didn't believe a regimen of speaking and listening practice would help. He needed to spend his available time, all of it, memorizing vocabulary and taking practice exams.

Qian wasn't a graduate student, so he didn't need the credits. Still, wouldn't his company disapprove?

"I haven't a company," he said. "My family paid for the course." He was, in effect, renting a dorm room for study hall. Marveling at his family's ability to afford the program, I mentally filed his movie star looks and optimistic air as signs of a privileged pedigree. Still, the GRE daunted him. Given the stakes of the exam he faced, he was falling back on what he knew best: rote memorization. I couldn't blame him.

"You don't think the oral practice will help you make connections in your brain?"

"No, I am sorry, not with this technical vocabulary." One hand hovered over his workbooks. "I think I need *this* for practice. Please," he pleaded, "not to tell the university."

"That's fine, it's between you and them. I won't say anything. But I won't be able to give you a certificate."

"Yes, it is okay. You see, it is at the end."

I moved toward the door. "Well, Qian Da Liang, you paid for the program, so you are always welcome. Especially to Free Talks." I shook his hand warmly. "Good luck, and drop in any time."

He surprised me by attending class the next two days, even though I'd tried to dispel his sense of guilt. Those were his last classroom appearances. Once in a while we saw each other around campus, occasions that called for diplomatic smiles: his reinforcing that he intended no offense, and mine reassuring that none was taken.

Toward the end of the semester the professionals class commandeered my apartment for a jiaozi party, and Qian joined in. As the women managed the cooking (mixing pork and vegetable filling, preparing dough, then assembling the dumplings to be steamed and fried), and as the men managed the television (soccer as usual), Qian and I caught up. He'd completed many workbooks, he said, but still had many more to go. The GRE was six weeks away.

I didn't remember his eyes searching so often for the right word. He fell back on Mandarin with his peers, a striking difference from the start of the semester, when he'd flaunted his superior English. Had he lost ground, or had their fluency overtaken his?

Either way, I couldn't help but admire Qian's determination, his single-minded focus so powerful it worked against his culture, propelling him out of the authoritative classroom structure and away from his peers.

. . .

BIRD SEED PILED. Chicken wire box tilted on the stick. Fishing line running to the bench. All set. He needs only to wait, and that is easy. He knows waiting.

The first pigeon pecks tentatively outside the trap. The old man waits. Another steps inside, but the first is in the way. He waits. More pigeons arrive, feeding in earnest now, a challenge for his eyes to track as they bob around and beneath the poised box. He doesn't want to crush a wing or foot, so he waits until all of the seed is gobbled. Most lose interest and lift away; three remain. Suddenly he sees an opportunity and yanks the fishing line – thud! The box drops and one pigeon startles off, leaving two trapped within, beating against the chicken wire.

The old man eases off the bench and shuffles forward. They're lively. He'd had money for only one whistle, so he must choose between them. Rimmed eyes flash on him as he inspects through the wire hexagons. Both appear healthy. He reaches through the cloth-covered hole at one end and seizes the feet of the nearest, his hand deft and sure (he did not always live in the city). Wings slapping, the pigeon rails against the exit, but he is patient, coaxing it out until its wings stretch back and clear.

He cups a hand over its back and coos softly. Then he kicks over the box and watches the other bird flee across the court and around the building.

Back at the bench he nestles the purple-gray sheen of its body between the thighs of his blue trousers. Palm pressing the downy torso, his fingers extend one spindly leather leg; his other hand positions the whistle band, then pinches it closed with pliers. A jiggle proves it unrestricting.

For a moment the old man cradles his bird and looks it in the face. One wide orange eye glares back. They will never again meet in this way.

Hands unfold – the pigeon dashes away in the direction of its fellow. As it picks up speed the old man catches the whistle's hollow tone just beginning to rise as the bird rounds the corner and is gone.

He sighs, sits, listens. And imagines.

For him nothing has changed – but in these first minutes everything has changed for his bird. It is chilled to the core by The Sound: the chiming metallic drone chasing it, relentless, no matter where it flies. It will swoop madly, desperate to flee the man-sound ripping the sky with its haunting wail. Called by the noise, other pigeons will flock in and follow, matching every swoop and dive with precision. Now it must outrun these pursuers as well as the sound.

After some hours his bird will succumb to fatigue, droop to the concrete, and discover the sound gone. Only the off-balancing leg band will remain. Yet when it lifts off the siren will rise again, resuming the chase.

In days his bird will no longer fear the noise emanating from the metal grip. In weeks it will come to expect the ringing upon takeoff, equating it with flight. In months it will no longer remember a time when the beat of its wings did *not* summon the entire flock – loyal subjects all – to air.

Wherever his bird soars, people on sidewalks will glance up, children will jump and point. Occasionally its wanderings will bring it across the court where it encountered the old man. Some days he will be there, sitting on the bench, squinting up into the sky and smiling. The magic he has wrought is small ... very small. But a day is better with it than without.

. . .

COMPOSITION: WHAT IS LIFE?

Perhaps, to live is a difficult thing. But in the world, everyone continue to live and makes a living for continuing to live.

Incoming snowball :: First snow

WINTER

Cold waking. Cold teaching. Cold eating. Cold sliding into bed.
Never had I been so constantly, unremittingly cold. Building interiors weren't *technically* freezing, but in winter the highest temperature my body felt was in the fifties, hour after hour, week after week. My body's thermal regulator wrote off extremities as too much effort. With Beijing at roughly the same latitude as New York City, the only hope of warmth lay in our hemisphere's eventual re-tilt toward the sun.

Cinder block classroom walls emanated cold like an icebox. My fingers, perpetually numb, had trouble holding whiteboard markers. Gloves made writing awkward, so I cut holes in a pair of socks and wore them on my hands, hoping even a thin second layer around the palms might coax a bit more blood into my digits.

"How do you stand it?" I asked my students.

"This is not so cold," they reassured. "We are north of the Yangtze River. We have heat. South of the Yangtze River the buildings have no heat."

"No heat at all? How far south is the Yangtze?"

"It is in the middle, but it is still very cold. And some parts of the river bend north."

"So they get heat."

"No," they laughed, "it is a law. These places are still south of the river, even though the river is north. So they have no heat."

Rarely did my apartment building have hot water. I checked the faucet compulsively. About twice a month I'd get lucky, whereupon I'd peel right out of my four layers (full-body thermals, t-shirt, turtleneck and sweater), scrub, and then yell "Hot water!" in the hallway so fellow teachers wouldn't miss it. Otherwise I subjected my skin to the ice-drizzling nozzle just once a week. This bathing regimen didn't stray far from the cultural norm – my students showered just once or twice a week, even in warm weather. Their dorms lacked showers, so they paid to use a separate facility on campus.

In the fall I wore a heavy leather jacket left behind by a predecessor. Then the real cold clamped down, and from the back of my closet I dug out an abandoned down coat – fluffy, impervious, practically toasty. I wasn't sure about the turquoise color, but hey, I was in China, free to wear what the Chinese wore.

So I thought. Students erupted into fits when they saw me.

"What's so funny?"

"Mistah Hobison, that color is only for girls!"

Oops.

Down coats were expensive – I doubted I could afford one on my Chinese salary, and I wasn't willing to dip into my U.S. cash reserve. So I returned to the leather jacket, along with about fifteen layers of thermals, t-shirts, long-sleeve shirts and sweatshirts, plus a knotted wool scarf. Not nearly as impregnable, but very manly.

Yes sir: cold and macho.

To think that I'd envisioned China as steamy rice paddies.

. . .

COMPOSITION: DESCRIBE A CHILDHOOD MEMORY.

I was six years old. One day in the winter, my mother gave me five cents

*Winter view from
my apartment*

for bathing. There was a bathing room in my village. If somebody paid five cents, he could bathed in here.

That time my family had a hard time because there was a bad crop in the year. Five cents were also important for my family's life. I was very glad to go to the bathing room with five cents.

Unfortunately, I lost the coin on my way.

I was very afraid and looked about for the coin carefully. I had not found it until it got dark. When I came back home like a culprit and told my mother this thing, she was very angry. She doubted my words and thought that I bought sugar-plum or other things. I related her I did not buy anything and the five cents coin was lost truly. However, my mother did not believe me and reprimanded me continually. I was quite sad for losing the coin and being blamed.

After the day, I always picked some useful things, such as papers and metals, from rubbish heaps, then sold them. In the winter, I gained fifty cents. I was very happy. When I gave the money to my mother and told her that the five cents were lost truly again, tears started from her eyes. She told me that she had forgot the thing and admitted that she was wrong.

Now I have come to Beijing from the village, but the incident has given me a strong and unforgettable impression.

. . .

THE BICYCLE LOT ATTENDANT told me something I didn't understand. No surprise there: I didn't get most of what anyone said. "Wo bu dong (*I don't understand*)," I replied, falling back on a phrase I used about ten times in every conversation.

"Ting bu dong," she replied.

Hunh. *Ting bu dong.* It sounded like my personal slogan *Wo bu dong. Wo* meant "I" – but who was *ting?*

She expected me to respond. I shook my head, smiled with embarrassment and repeated, "Wo bu dong."

"Ting bu dong," she said.

Ting again. So it was important enough to repeat. I searched my limited vocabulary, trying to puzzle it out. *Ting, ting …* what could she be saying? Another head shake, another sheepish apology: "Wo bu dong."

"Ting bu dong," she insisted.

This was becoming humiliating. "Dui bu qi," I apologized. "Wo bu dong, zai jian." I stepped away with her muttering "Ting bu dong" behind me.

At home I checked the dictionary. *Ting* meant "to hear." *Hear not understand?* That didn't make sense.

At Da Shi Tang I asked my students, who explained: "*Ting bu dong*, it means 'I can hear you, but I do not understand your words.'"

"She didn't understand me? I said *Wo bu dong*. I say that all the time – everyone understands me."

"No no no no no!" they laughed. "You said *Wo bu dong*, it means 'I cannot understand you,' as in 'I cannot hear your voice.' Rather you should say *Ting bu dong*."

I'd been using the wrong phrase in every Mandarin conversation I'd ever had. For months. *Ting bu dong*. The bicycle attendant had been correcting my grammar.

And all I could parrot back was *Wo bu dong* …

. . .

No, NO, THIS IS WRONG," Rebecca grumbled over the box I'd prepared for mailing. "I will come back."

What could be wrong? I wanted to ship a care package of cookies, old *Reader's Digest*s and funny tourist dong xi to a fellow teacher having a rough time in another city. I'd wrapped a box in grocery-brown paper; then, not trusting my Chinese handwriting, I'd asked one of my students to address it. A single look earned her disapproval.

Minutes later Rebecca returned with a coarse pillowcase, a needle and thread. Gesturing at my box she instructed, "Take everything out." She repacked the items into the pillowcase.

"What are you doing?" I was bewildered. "That isn't sturdy. Things will break."

"No, it will be okay. It must be this, or they will not send it."

"Why?"

Stamps on airmail letter

"They must check it." Evidently packages received a touch inspection through fabric to ensure ... what?

She stitched the opening shut, then wrote the address in ballpoint pen, flattening the fabric on a hard surface within. "There," she proclaimed. It looked like a floppy Santa sack, but she was satisfied. I strapped it to the back of my bicycle and pedaled to the post office.

. . .

IN THE CINDER BLOCK BUILDING, down the dim corridor, through the hollow wood door on the left, find the post office. One room packed with sniffling patrons. Dusty light. Worn wooden table in the middle. At the back, a narrow counter beneath a small clerk window.

Hand your package through the bodies crowding the window, where weight and destination are checked, cost determined, stamps sold. Then back out and approach the table. The stamps aren't sticky, not even lickable. You need glue.

Anchored atop the table is the glue pot. Use one of the metal-handled brushes slumped inside. Dab your stamps, press them into place, return the brush. Take a moment to consider the pot.

It has endured here for decades, thick globs cascading from rim to table like the flow of rock in a cave. On closer look no actual pot is discernible within those opaque folds; perhaps the pot itself is made of glue. Patrons ceased worrying long ago about spillage. Indeed its organic, beeswax shape has inspired one after another, dozens upon hundreds, upon thousands, all engaging in the most subtle of rebellions: glopping freely, almost religiously – anonymous signatures added to the communal construct.

. . .

SNOWBALLS CROSSED CULTURES. Snow angels didn't.

As we celebrated the year's first snow with a spirited snowball fight, I dropped into a drift and swung my arms and legs around. Students guffawed.

"No, look," I said, leaping out of my artistry.

That's when I realized the problem with snow angels: they don't resemble anything unless you know what you're looking for.

My students sure didn't. "Don't you see the wings, the dress?" I pointed. "Look, right there, it's an angel!" The word meant nothing to them. Their teacher had simply wiggled in the snow like a weirdo.

Beijingers impressed me by riding their bicycles in the snow. It took a bit of extra caution but beat walking, so I picked up the skill myself.

And yes, they made snowmen, too – only they didn't call them that. They were snow pandas.

. . .

THE CAPITALS OF CHINA AND AMERICA shared an unusual trait: a low skyline. Buildings in Washington D.C. squat beneath the height of the U.S. Capitol; those in Beijing ducked under a law requiring anything over six stories to have an elevator with a human operator – effectively stunting building heights and strengthening legs.

The saddest job I saw was that of elevator operator: small, fresh-out-of-school girl shut in a metal box, away from fresh air and daylight, rising and descending all day just to press the button for your floor. Such was government-guaranteed employment.

At university gates, guards stood at attention, bored, rocking on their soles. Teams of men stooped along highway shoulders, snipping grass with scissors. Women sat in narrow glass booths at subway stations to keep watch in case the escalator broke down.

In Forbidden City buildings, employees slouched over little radios, huddled in their coats against the winter freeze. They didn't speak, didn't glance up, just kept each hand pressed between stool and thigh, swaying slightly. How they must have felt on their first day of work – "The Forbidden City! Glorious place to report every day!" – only for the daily grind to creep in, leaching motivation month by month until eventually they wished to be anywhere else.

Once assigned to a work unit, could a person later be transferred else-

Six-story city

where? A few of my grad students bemoaned their major, forestry, in part because they were stuck with it. They either accepted a government-funded education in forestry or returned to a life of peasantry. Did the Communist Party consider grass clippers, elevator button pushers, exhibit minders to be placed for life?

The choice between mindless sinecure or abject poverty was a no-brainer, especially if one had a family to support.

Still – what uninspiring solutions.

. . .

THEY'D HEARD OF CHRISTMAS, of course, but not Thanksgiving, Easter or Halloween. A bit of holiday fun was due.

During the week I designated Christmas, we made cards and sang carols (their favorites were "Rudolph" and the "Glo-o-o-o-o-oria" refrain). Another week we mimicked Easter by dyeing, hunting for, and tossing eggs. I wasn't permitted to say much about these holidays' origins, so that was about as deep as those lessons ran.

When I found pumpkins at Wudaokou, our Halloween week turned into an orange gloppy mess. We carved jack-o'-lanterns, whipped up crude paper/crayon masks, and told ghost stories. In the one Chinese story I recall, a floating head with pasty flesh and dangling red hair haunted a hotel in Jiayuguan, Tail of the Great Wall.

I struggled to distinguish Thanksgiving from the many Chinese family- and food-oriented holidays. Lacking turkey, stuffing, cranberry sauce and mashed potatoes, I didn't feel I could provide an adequate experience.

Highway sweeper outside Xian

So it was that my favorite holiday received a mere historical overview: pilgrims, ships, and a quest for self-determination – a quest I hoped would resonate.

. . .

ONCE A WEEK I reserved the TV room, lined up sixty-odd chairs, and treated students to such cultural icons as *Star Wars* and *Ghostbusters*, *Goonies* and *Tootsie*. And *Sixteen Candles*, where they found the slow dancing hilarious. *Jaws* – part thrillcoaster, part snapshot of small-town American beach life – became an instant hit.

Their all-time favorite, though, was *A Christmas Story*. "We want more movies like this," they demanded. "We want the real life American movies."

"You don't understand," I explained, "there aren't any more movies like that. *A Christmas Story* is the best ever made. Besides, America's not like that anymore. That was the 1940's."

"But this is the movie we like. Not ghosts or UFOs." Throughout December they asked for *A Christmas Story* each week. I continued showing new features on Fridays, and reserved the room on different days for reruns of Ralphie's Red Ryder quest.

Before showing any film I screened it and took notes so I could pre-teach helpful vocabulary and cultural elements. In my preview of *A Christmas Story* two scenes made me nervous.

One was the famous restaurant scene near the end. Their turkey devoured by the Bumpus hounds, Ralphie's family eats out at a Chinese restaurant (the only place open on Christmas Day), where the waiters "fa-ra-ra" their way through "Deck the Halls" and guillotine a roasted duck at the table.

Masks and jack-o'-lanterns

How would my students handle such stereotypes?

I winced the first time it played, but seeing their own culture appear in a classic American film made them feel exquisitely honored. It suggested *they* might have a place in America. Besides, "fa-ra-ra" invited them to laugh at their own English struggles.

The other worrisome scene came in the first five minutes. Actually it was just one line: when little brother Randy won't eat, his mother goads him with the familiar guilt trip, "There are starving people in China!" The scene was priceless, a faithful reenactment of nightly dining table antics across the United States. But that line!

China was a living contradiction – a proud nation with an inferiority complex. The birthplace of paper, gunpowder and silk, somehow China had allowed other nations to pull ahead. As they opened to the rest of the world, then, just how far behind the Chinese had slipped became apparent. It was a matter of national face. They were unsettled.

How would my students react, hearing their country bandied about as poverty's poster child?

No way would the line go unnoticed. My students would ask, and I would need to explain. What would I say? How would I inform real, live people I knew and loved, people who'd been such gracious hosts to me, that the homeland they viewed as a global superpower was, in 1993, still considered by many a Third World nation?

I couldn't do it, couldn't think of a single explanation that would work. Maybe the cold hard truth would be best, making them face Maoism's consequences square on. But I didn't want to shock them with a rude intervention – I just wanted them to enjoy *A Christmas Story*, which would be impossible

Easter festivities

after a damaging first impression.

So I punted.

I showed the scene. By the end of the semester I must have showed that scene, and the entire movie, five times. And every single time, right as the Starving China line neared, I chose that moment to step to the TV, thumb the volume down to zero and ask, "Can everyone see okay? Is it loud enough? It's okay? Good."

Maybe they caught on, maybe they didn't. If nothing else, they must have considered it strange that their teacher checked the sound only during this particular movie, and always during the same few seconds.

Of course the gesture was futile. They would see the film again at some point in the lives. But by then I'd be half a globe away.

Besides, Chinese censors would have done their work, and had the line removed.

. . .

COMPOSITION: WHAT IS YOUR FAVORITE AMERICAN HOLIDAY?

I'm not sure how American spent their holiday in Christmastide. But I'm sure I will receive a present from Santa Claus if I stay in America at Christmas Eve.

. . .

ACCORDING TO MY STUDENTS, China was atheist, America Christian – gross generalities that nevertheless inspired a tightrope dance of questions. Did I know the Bible? Did I visit church? And what about Waco? (When Waco hit the headlines that year, Chinese media snapped it up as proof of U.S. hypocrisy on human rights.)

On Sundays I attended Beijing International Christian Fellowship (BICF), a United Nations-esque worship service that met in the lecture hall of a foreign corporation's headquarters. I met people from Italy, Benin, Bulgaria, Togo, South Korea, Germany. Those from Francophone nations wore earpieces for on-the-spot translation. Many students from African nations pursued science and engineering degrees for a fraction of the cost of higher education in America or Europe; they just needed to spend an initial year immersing themselves in Mandarin.

Conspicuously *un*represented at BICF was China itself – nationals were strictly forbidden. As late as 2009 the BICF website posted this disclaimer on its main page: "Due to local government regulations, the Fellowship is open to foreign passport holders only. Please bring a photo ID that proves foreign citizenship. Thank you for your cooperation."

The Chinese weren't banned from all worship, only the unregulated sort. The government operated a handful of local churches for the religiously inclined – churches that kept records on attendees.

On Christmas Eve I visited one of these churches, sitting politely though I understood few words. The straight liturgical service was videotaped, both altar and congregation. I wondered how worshippers felt about putting their faces on permanent record in a nation with a history of imprisoning Christians.

One of my students asked if I owned a Chinese translation of the Bible. "I would like to read the Bible," he said, "to know about it for myself. But to buy a Bible I have to register my name." Who could blame him for hesitating?

. . .

IN MID-DECEMBER greeting cards flocked through Wudaokou, perching on strings slung across stalls. *Merry Christmas, Best Wishes*, the messages read, accompanied by images of birds and flowers, umbrellas and children. *May the joys of this season be with you throughout the coming year.*

The Chinese didn't celebrate Christmas. They just gave each other the cards.

I received a few of these cards from my students. *Please accept my best and sincerest wishes for the Christmas*, one wrote inside. Another: *May Christmas brighten your prospects wherever you go.*

That year Christmas landed on a Saturday, a morning numb and quiet. I ate oatmeal, skimmed an old *Reader's Digest*, checked for hot water (Santa

New Year's Eve party

hadn't brought any). Around midday I joined the other American teachers plus the lone German in our building for a potluck lunch. We exchanged gifts of dong xi we'd found at Wudaokou: tart fruit candy, paper cuttings, hand massage balls, figurines, commemorative coins. And, of course, Chinese Christmas cards.

Who printed them? Why were they exchanged? When did it all begin? One more cultural mystery to chuckle at, and enjoy.

. . .

COMPOSITION: DESCRIBE YOUR FAMILY.

> *I'm sad of talking about my family. My father, a kind-hearted and hard-working peasant, died of disease four months ago. When he was alive, he was strict with his children. He always encouraged me to study harder so as to become a useful man in the future. I will never forget him!*

. . .

IN THE MIDDLE OF A DA SHI TANG MEAL I adjusted my stool. Only the seat plank lifted – then came down on the tip of my finger as I sat, slicing away a hunk of flesh. My hand dripped red.

Lacking napkins or tissues, students offered me a wad of paper meal tickets to staunch the blood. I declined. I also declined the subsequent offer of a silk handkerchief. The bleeding wasn't slowing, so I removed one shoe and sock, wrapped the sock around my finger, and raised my hand above my head.

All concern for my health evaporated as my tablemates fell over themselves in laughter.

Elevating an injury? They'd never heard of it (Americans sure were superstitious). Plus, removing a shoe in public was rude enough – they'd never *imagined* taking off a sock.

"But it's okay for you to do it," they concluded, wiping away tears, "because it's just your American way."

. . .

OUTSIDE CLASS, students sometimes forgot me as they chatted in Mandarin. I'd listen intently, trying to pick out familiar words.

Every few minutes someone would notice me again, giggle and ask, "Do you know what we're talking about?" I rarely did. Still, the cadence and speed of their conversations fascinated me. I guessed at jokes based on expressions and tones, and occasionally asked for the meaning of recurring words: "*Zao gao* shen me yisi (*What does* zao gao *mean*)?"

One day I caught them off guard. In a particularly rambunctious discussion they kept repeating one word: *mai ke.* So I asked: "*Mai ke* shen me yisi?"

They fell quiet, blushing. No one answered.

Intrigued, I pressed: "*Mai ke* shen me yisi?"

A few squealed into their palms.

"Come on, tell me," I insisted.

Finally Sarah confessed: "It is *your* name."

Aha: *Mike* = "mai ke." The sneaks! Knowing I'd recognize my Chinese name, they'd switched to a code word for me – yet I'd stumbled onto it by luck.

I never heard *mai ke* after that. No doubt they switched to some other term ("curly hair" or "big nose") that I failed to pick out.

. . .

COMPOSITION: EXPLAIN A MISTAKE YOU WILL NEVER FORGET.

> When I was in college, I had a good friend. His name is Feng Shen. One day, I was tired after hard work. So I wanted to relax. I decided to go to movie with Feng Shen. When I got to his dormitory, he was sitting on the bed. I said to him: "Let's go to movie." I wanted to relax. In that time I can't notice his face. He said: "No, I can't do." "Go, go." I shaked his hand and went out the door.
>
> After saw movie, we walk along the street. Feng Shen turn to me. "Nothing is more sad than my feeling now. My sister wrote to me and told my mother is dead because of hard work."
>
> I was amazing. "Oh my God. I really sorry. I'm wrong. I mustn't invite you to go to movie. I . . . "
>
> "Don't explain and say sorry. We are good friends. You needn't say more. I forgive you," he said.
>
> "This is my stupidest thing that I ever did," I sadly said.

. . .

WHAT DOES THAT MEAN?" Fred asked during a movie.

"What?"

"That." He hunched his shoulders up to his ears.

"You don't do it in China?"

"No, what is it?"

"It means *I don't know*. You don't know and you don't really care."

Everyone tried it.

"No, just once," I said. "Don't keep doing it, that looks funny. Here: what time is it?"

"Ten-forty."

"No, practice doing *I don't know*. You don't know what time it is. Are you ready? What time is it?"

They shrugged. It looked funny without the noise.

"Okay, we also make a noise when we do it, like this: uhduhknuh. Everyone say it after me: uh-duh-knuh." I exaggerated the inflection, making it sound even sillier than it already did.

"Uh-duh-knuh!" They giggled.

"It sounds like *I don't know*. Idontknow. Uhduhknuh." I paused, then asked, "So what time is it?"

Sixteen sets of shoulders shrugged as they voiced: "Uhduhknuh."

"Perfect – you'll fit right in."

. . .

BY BICYCLE, BUS AND SUBWAY it took 45 minutes to reach the McDonald's near Tiananmen Square – two floors, eight cashiers, teeming with people.

I'd invited my student Johnny to a meal in order to discuss hiring him as a Mandarin tutor. Glassy-eyed before the glowing menu, he asked, "What do I order?" This was a bit odd, as the choices were printed in Chinese and accompanied by pictures. I explained several items, then told him the quintessential McDonald's experience was a burger. We each ordered a Quarter

McDonald's near Tiananmen Square

Pounder.

Our fries cooled as we circled with our trays, searching for two contiguous seats. All around us customers were trying to eat with their hands without exactly eating with their hands, fingertips only. Some attacked their burgers with knife and fork. Unable to find a free table, Johnny and I settled on tandem seats across from two strangers.

"What's this?" he asked, inspecting a packet.

"Ketchup," I answered. "See?" I pointed at the Chinese label. His expression indicated it didn't help. "It's a paste made from tomatoes," I said, repeating what I'd always heard but frowning at the sudden realization that ketchup didn't really taste like tomatoes. "But it's salty, or tangy or something." I gave up.

"What do you do with it?"

"Put in on your burger."

Thanks to our side-by-side arrangement, Johnny couldn't watch me easily. I glanced over to see him squirting ketchup on the *top* of his top bun. He sensed something was wrong, then solved it by eating the top bun first, like a piece of toast with jelly. This left the burger proper, which he consumed with thumbs on the bottom bun, fingertips on the beef.

Of course his mistakes were my fault – I'd failed to coach him through each step. You don't realize the many cultural assumptions entailed in something as basic as eating a hamburger until you see an outsider knock right through them. Johnny's topless burger made me wonder how badly I was blundering through Beijing without even realizing it.

I feared McDonald's was a bust, but as we left Johnny said, "I like this food better than Pizza Hut. I like especially the potatoes."

"The fries."

"Yes, I like especially the potatoes fries."

Kunming Lake at Yihe Yuan :: Apartment view

ALONE

End of the semester. Every American teacher I knew headed south by train to Hong Kong. I stayed behind.

I'd traveled to China to experience life from a different perspective, yet my situation – salary, apartment – exceeded that of ordinary Chinese citizens. Skipping off to a British territory for the holidays felt like an additional flamboyance, so I chose to play local instead.

Johnny, a Beijing native, had agreed to a role reversal: he would tutor me in Mandarin two hours a day, five days a week. At first he insisted on teaching me for free, but through persistent negotiation I hiked his hourly rate up to something I hoped was fair.

My student turned out to be quite the taskmaster. He proposed a diet of forty new words each day, yielding a working vocabulary of one thousand words. Did the Chinese study English at such a feverish pace? Despite his assurances, I doubted my ability to keep up.

As the weeks progressed – practicing in workbooks, cooking my own pitiful meals, poking by bicycle into Beijing's nooks – the cold impacted me, as did the isolation, brown dustiness, boredom. Yet none of these circumstances caught me off guard as much as seeing no white faces around me. Ever.

One day Johnny and I toured the Forbidden City. I used my work unit card to buy a regular ticket, rather than the more expensive foreigner's ticket. Later, as we crowded at the entrance, the guard asked for proof of my eligibility to pay Chinese prices. Again I produced my work unit card, but – yes, this is strange – I wondered how he knew to stop me.

Imagine: a white person surprised that a Chinese person could tell he wasn't Chinese. Had I lost my mind?

For months I'd been asked, on buses and subways, if I was American, Canadian, European, Australian. Other guesses included Greek, Uyghur (a minority group in western China), Jewish, Puerto Rican, Indian. One glance proved I was anything *but* Chinese. So why didn't I expect this guard to identify me as a waiguoren?

Total immersion weighed on my psyche. Wherever I went, the Chinese noted a break in continuity: numerous Asian faces bundled against the cold, and one white face. But I saw no such break, only a single collection of Asian faces, all bundled up, which matched *my* sensory impression of being bundled up. From inside my head, I seemed the same as everyone else – a perspective that eventually brought me to a point of momentary forgetfulness.

I watched a ton of Chinese TV during those weeks. I practiced forming Chinese characters, trying to shed the juvenile look of my handwriting. I ate alone in my kitchen – oatmeal, rice, jiaozi.

Is it any wonder I dreamt my face was becoming Chinese?

Sound asleep one night, I looked in the mirror and noticed my brow and forehead flattening, my nose broadening, cheekbones widening.

In the dream I was thrilled.

I didn't regret my identity or seek to change nationality. The constant sense of *difference* must have pressured me subconsciously into wanting to conform.

Flash forward to today. I will confess that at times, reading articles about minority issues in America, I am tempted to ask, "Must ethnicity *always* be an issue? Why not be American, simply American, like everyone else?" Our society's road out of prejudice has been long, our progress slow, and I admit

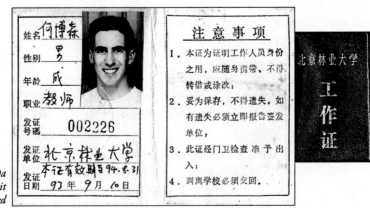

Lin Da work unit card

this can make me tired. But of course such questions never occurred to me in China, where I was a minority myself!

My identity as an outsider placed an asterisk on every interaction. A vendor charged me too much*^{Taking Advantage of a Waiguoren}. A passerby helped me find the right store*^{Showing Hospitality to a Waiguoren}. The bus attendant took my money without a second glance*^{Treated the Same As Everyone Else, Rather Than As a Waiguoren}.

No amount of fatigue over my identity would have nullified it. For better or worse, the minority element always factored in.

Here's the rub. Every moment in China I knew I could catch a flight home and blend back in with everyone else, but minorities in America have no easy retreat. They're already home.

. . .

My ACCENT was coming along nicely. Johnny was pleased. "You should study hard," he encouraged. "You could become a newscaster."

"Shut up."

"Zhen de (*Really*)." He told me about a white Canadian who'd mastered Mandarin so well a TV station recruited him as a novelty newscaster. Actors trained him to mimic facial expressions and mannerisms that, combined with his precise accent, gave viewers the bizarre spectacle of a white person more properly Chinese than they were.

I took in hours of TV every day, hoping to improve my inflections and mannerisms. Watching show after show I didn't understand felt admittedly odd. My first hint of breakthrough occurred during a soap opera set in ancient times. In the midst of a lovers' quarrel, an armored warrior proclaimed to his silken maiden, "Wo ai ni! Wo ai ni!" I jolted. Unlike the tidbits I

Satellite TV dish among hutongs

103

gleaned elsewhere, these lines dripped with meaning: *I love you!*

The Chinese watched a lot of TV; they seemed to live for it. A few of the humbler hutongs around Lin Da, with thin glass panes and charcoal bricks stacked outside for heat, sported satellite dishes. When I visited students' families we typically ended up watching TV – news, movies, soccer.

Language learning aside, I'm not much of a TV person, so at first this habit struck me as foreign, unusual. But the more I thought about it, America was just the same.

. . .

I KNEW CHINA WOULD GIVE ME another perspective on the world, on human beings, on myself.

But on the inside of my mouth?

Take the letter J: jaguar, jelly, jump. Nothing to it – except that Mandarin had two forms of J, each a distinct consonant.

The *jian* in *zai jian* ("goodbye") was pronounced with tongue tip brushing the back of the bottom teeth along the gumline, its middle arched against the roof of the mouth. Try this until you can make a J-type sound.

Now compare that to the *zhong* in *Zhong Guo* ("China"), spoken with the tongue curled up and back, toward the back of the mouth. This sound should be harsher, with a hint of an R.

Switch back and forth between these tongue positions, each time making a J sound. Hear the difference?

Other consonants were based on similar shifts in tongue placement. Try the SH sounds in *xie xie* ("thank you") and *shi* ("to be"): X with tongue tip forward and down against the bottom teeth, SH with tongue up and back. Or the CH sounds in *qing* ("please") and *Chang Cheng* ("Great Wall"): Q forward, CH back.

Would anyone notice if I blurred these consonants the American way? I tried at first; it sounded as wrong to them as "fa-ra-ra."

I'd never heard any syllable as strange as *ri* – again with the tongue raised up and back, but spoken as though the R sound was pronounced backwards.

Toughest for me was the letter C. Make a soft TS sound (as in "bits") with the tongue tip forward and down, the middle arched against the top front teeth. Not too difficult – except that every time I tried it, Johnny corrected me.

"No no no, listen." He'd make the C sound several times, gesturing toward his mouth.

"C, C, C," I'd repeat.

"No no, look this," he'd say, "look my tongue." Again he'd pronounce, "C, C, C."

"C, C, C," I'd repeat.

"No no no, not C, *C*. Like this: C, C, C."

"C, C." Deep breath. "C!"

"No, look close. C, C."

"C, C."

"No."

And so on. Try as I could, I never made the sound to his satisfaction — nor did I have any clue as to how my C differed from his.

. . .

ON THE SIDEWALK men of mixed ages squatted near a chessboard, slapping down pieces with gong fu flavor. It reminded me of a scene from a New York City park. Games like this one were corporate affairs, not so much a contest between two minds as a collaborative exploration of strategies. Spectators and combatants shared ideas for moves as long as words could keep up with fingers.

Xianqi, or Chinese chess, looked nothing like Chinese checkers, the farcical colored marbles we know in America. Similar in gameplay to our chess (what they called "international chess"), Xiangqi used a few different pieces and movements. Beside each horse was an elephant that moved in 2x2 squares. The generals (kings) had two close guards but no queens, were restricted to a palace (3x3 box), and were forbidden from facing one another. Cannons attacked only *over* another piece, never directly. All pieces were flat disks printed with Chinese characters. A "river" ran across the middle of the

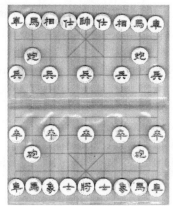

My magnetic Xianqi (Chinese chess) set — 9x10, not 8x8, with pieces sitting on intersections rather than squares

board, affecting the movement of soldiers (pawns) and elephants.

More subtle differences existed; it took me a while to absorb them all. I found Xiangqi more intricate than international chess, with additional variables and constraints in both offense and defense. Early in the year I bought a set, asked students to explain the rules, and took a drubbing in actual gameplay. Then I staged mock battles against myself until I felt ready to challenge them again. I won a few games, lost several, and generally amazed the very men who'd taught me to distinguish one piece from another. Fundamentally Xianqi and international chess were the same, and I could hold my own on a chessboard.

So I thought, until Xiao Ming stomped me.

Short, unkempt, a natural comedian, Xiao Ming worked as a building superintendent for a reason: he was no scholar. Most of every day he either entertained friends in his efficiency beside our building entrance, or watched TV. So when he noticed the Xiangqi set on my dining table and offered to play, I hemmed and hawed, declining for weeks … until my winter alone, when I had nothing better to do. I didn't expect much.

The table nullified our height difference, and as we focused on the miniature battlefield between us Xiao Ming's demeanor chiseled into that of a grave commander. Early on I captured a handful of pieces and placed him in some quick checks, but I wound up reeling from a multipronged attack. The match was entirely his, my moves selected for me by the dwindling gaps in his offense.

"Hen hao (*Very good*)," he said when it was over, lazy smile returning. He was being overly gracious. "Chong lai ma (*Again*)?"

Sucker: the next game was a shameful rout. Unaware of what I'd done differently between the two bouts, I burned with embarrassment.

I'd seen a whole different side of Xiao Ming, a complexity I hadn't suspected. How often did he play? When? I'd never seen him near a Xiangqi board, but obviously he was skilled – enough to make me realize the students I'd felt so proud of beating were just novices like me.

From time to time Xiao Ming, vacuuming my apartment, would offer to play again. My excuses must have amused him. He'd insist it was okay, we could just play a quick game for fun, but I'd insist right back that it wasn't that at all, that I really was too busy or whatever.

Then in the evenings I'd play my students again.

I got a little better, I think … just never to the point I felt I could take on the general again.

. . .

Picture a map of the world. Americas on the left, Asia and Australia on the right, skinny Atlantic down the middle. Right?

Not in China.

They fixed their homeland at the middle, making the wide Pacific the most prominent feature – and shoving the Americas off to the side, where they were distorted by edge curvature.

These maps matched China's self-concept. Every nation indulges in a little solipsism, but the Chinese embedded theirs right in their national name: *Zhong Guo* 中国, "Center Country." Note the obvious symbolism of the character *zhong*: 中.

I expected the term for America, *Mei Guo* 美国, to have a slighting meaning, like "Somewhere Over There Country." How pleasant to discover that *mei* meant "beautiful."

. . .

Clerks bombarded me with sales pitch as soon as I stepped foot in a store. I comprehended little, but the sales talk still persisted as long as I did. This went on for six months.

Then: magic.

The sole customer in one store, I was being harangued by two clerks when a woman entered. They redirected their barrage at her, but the woman muttered a phrase and they fell quiet.

Immediately I parsed her words. *Wo kan yi kan.* What did it mean? *Wo* meant "I," and *yi* sounded like "one." *Kan* was unfamiliar to me. Still, the phrase was potent. I left that store and entered the next one for no purpose other than to test the phrase. I crossed the threshold; the sales pitch commenced.

"Wo kan yi kan," I said.

It stopped.

I used that phrase for weeks before remembering to check the dictionary. *Kan* meant "to look." *Wo kan yi kan* = "I look one look" = "I'm just looking."

My vocabulary may have been limited, but I learned most of my words this way – like a baby, absorbing bits of speech from real situations and using them to accomplish real purposes, sometimes without fully understanding their meaning.

No wonder, then, that fifteen years later I recall many Mandarin phrases without effort.

. . .

MAO RED BOOK?" street salesmen asked. Surely you, Lao Wai, needed a copy of Mao's political manifesto. How had you made it so long without one?

I wondered if these little books were printed in English. Did they sell to waiguoren as a means of Communist proselytizing? Or was this simple (and ironic) capitalistic opportunism?

Chairman Mao Zedong, architect of Communist China, had expelled both Chinese aristocrats and Japanese invaders. More than a statesman, Mao had been deemed a visionary, a near deity, even a sex symbol. Many of my female students carried trading cards with plump old Mao on one side, dashing twenty-something Mao on the other. "You really think he's good looking?" I asked. They practically fanned themselves.

Twenty years deceased, Mao's shadow lingered in everyday life. Many of the elderly continued to wear Mao uniforms – plain blue trousers, plain blue jacket, plain blue hat. They carried their birdcages to parks, hung them on branches and listened to their parakeets calling frenetically to one another.

Old or young, nearly all men smoked. To bolster the economy Mao had popularized smoking as something akin to a civic duty. He smoked; he told patriots to smoke. Instant tobacco industry.

Despite Communism's ideal of gender equity, women did *not* smoke. One exception was my student Esther, a particularly artistic and free spirit. Whenever I spotted her smoking it was hard for me not to stare at such an uncommon sight. Why hadn't Mao urged women to smoke as well? Passing up higher tobacco revenues by upholding a double standard seemed out of character.

Every Saturday my students attended "political class." I didn't know where it was held or what it covered. One Saturday I noticed workers in a restaurant listening to a somber voice over a loudspeaker. They sat at tables

Coin commemorating Mao's 100th birthday, which occurred (posthumously) on December 26, 1993

taking notes, staring at their shoes or reading the newspaper. Was *that* political class – piped lectures?

At the end of the semester my students mentioned that they'd taken their political final exam. "Was it difficult?" I asked.

"No," they laughed. "It was true/false."

"*All* true/false?"

"Yes."

A political exam with nothing but true/false questions: what could be more Politically Correct?

. . .

MAO GREW FAT – a sign of prosperity. Fat was good. In a country of little means, fatness indicated vitality. Yet the hypocrisy of Mao's fatness seemed lost on his own resource-strapped subjects. Mao represented the nation, and if Mao was fat, the nation must be thriving, even if individual citizens were not. Such was Communism. Between the two, old Mao or young, it was the rotund likeness that hung at the Forbidden City gate.

In earlier decades, homes and public buildings had displayed Mao shrines: portraits attended by tassels, calligraphy scrolls and candles. In 1993 I came across few such displays. Times were changing, the economy had begun to boom, and everyday life accelerated, leaving little time to dwell on the past.

I did visit Mao in his mausoleum. You can, too. It's hard to miss – ornate building skirted by steps and security gobbling up a third of Tiananmen Square. Stand in line for an hour and you, too, can be ushered past the glass case of Mao's preserved remains, paying hushed ten-second respect from fifteen feet away.

He looked like a wax dummy. No surprise there: the man died in 1972. Still, if long-term preservation made a real body look artificial, why not stick with a dummy? Though I didn't dare breathe such skepticism to my students, they flirted with it themselves. "There are two bodies," Rebecca explained. "One is real, one is not real. They are under the ground, perhaps one hundred of feet down. Each day they raise one body for looking. You do not know if it is the real body."

If this were true, the government would have no motivation to risk displaying Mao's real body. I suspected it was a myth to create an illusion of authenticity, helping common citizens connect with a leader who had cared for each and every one of them … as he grew fat.

How very Communist.

How very Mao.

. . .

I AM, YOU ARE, IT IS. Not easy from an outsider's perspective – none of these conjugations resembles the infinitive *to be.*

What a relief, then, to learn a language without conjugation! Here's the Mandarin *shi* ("to be"):

	Singular	Plural
First Person	shi	shi
Second Person	shi	shi
Third Person	shi	shi

Past tense was equally simple – speakers merely told when the action occurred, such as *zuotian* ("yesterday"), or threw in a marker like *le* for a completed action.

That's not to suggest Mandarin lacked its own landmines. Hundreds of idioms encapsulated cultural history in little four-character combinations impossible to puzzle out. *Ma ma hu hu* literally meant "horse horse tiger tiger" but was properly translated "so-so."

Johnny enjoyed stumping me with literal idioms. He'd scribble on a slip of paper, then grin as I'd read: "Guard tree wait rabbit draw biscuit fill hungry."

"No," he'd chuckle, "it means *If you do not work hard, you will eat only dreams.*"

. . .

AS A CHILD I heard that fish grow in proportion to the size of their containers. Larger tank, larger fish.

Probably I had that confused with houseplants, but anyway.

Patty, an American teacher who lived down the hall, kept three goldfish in a puny bowl that flashed with territorial disputes, the largest nipping relentlessly at its bowlmates. In the winter she left me to care for them as she traveled.

With hot water almost as rare as an empty bus seat, it wasn't as though my bathtub was seeing much use. My plan was simple: keep 'em in the tub and feed 'em like mad. When Patty returned five weeks later she'd find her fish twice as big.

I placed their bowl on the dry porcelain bottom of my tub and cranked the faucet. I wondered how they'd react to a line of water creeping *outside* their tank.

They didn't.

The water reached their bowl's rim and cascaded over. Tub and bowl were now one body; soon the fish would have enough clearance to pass over. I leaned in close, anticipating the moment when they would realize they could glide out.

They didn't.

Because their bowl wasn't oxygenated they had a habit of surfacing to gulp air. This they continued, rising until parallel with the former water surface, then descending as though satisfied. The tub continued filling, water lifting higher above their bowl. I'd granted them a domain forty times the breadth of their cramped space, yet they circled stubbornly within the familiar, the largest still nipping with territorial aggression.

With the tub filled to the rim, I stopped the faucet and hunkered down to watch. Surely they'd figure it out. Eventually?

Maybe not. Five minutes passed, whittling my grand mischief down to a sad non-event. Boredom left room for philosophy. Was I like these fish? Did I possess greater freedoms, a broader realm than I dared conceive, yet fix myself within the tight, dysfunctional bubble of the status quo?

No time to speculate: one of the smaller fish had risen – and paused. Momentum kept it gliding upward, and as its eyes passed the bowl's rim I could swear they bulged. It gave the slightest wriggle, rose further, stopped; wriggled again, stopped; then resolutely ascended until it surfaced, where it happily gulped air and turned horizontal.

Now it coasted, pausing every so often as if expecting the bowl's invisible edge. When it finally did reach the porcelain boundary it began to wander aimlessly, basking in its new environs. Eventually the little explorer discovered the wall of its former bowl, convex now instead of concave, and looked in on the dumb chaps still inside. What must they have thought, seeing their bowlmate *outside* the glass?

Minutes later the other small fish emerged like the first, through slow investigative wriggles. Once out, it sought the other, either for reassurance or to share in wonderment.

Having won sole occupancy of its long-coveted prize, the thickish bully clung to that pathetic trophy longest of all, reluctant to acknowledge a freer world. After a long interval it finally joined the others, twitching around the tub as if with a body tic.

Patty's fish enjoyed the tub and extra feedings the entire vacation. Only once a week, when my own grunge drove me toward an icy shower, did I pull them out. Afterwards I'd reposition their bowl, refill the tub, and keep dousing them with food.

Sadly, the plan didn't work: if Patty's fish were larger when she returned, she didn't notice. Worse, I had to return them to their tiny bowl. I wondered if they were better off having experienced liberation only to lose it. The larger one did seem more tolerant of his fellows.

That the bully was last out still pleases me. Perhaps aggression correlates with a lack of imagination. I wonder about the world's bullies, dictators such as Lenin, Pinochet, Mao Zedong. Despite their profound impact on millions of lives, I suspect their worldviews of being fundamentally too flat.

If *we* are all that we know – if we acknowledge no greater mysteries, no inexplicable wonders beyond our understanding – then the world shrinks around us, allowing our needs and appetites to outweigh those of any other, turning us into little despots.

Human nature *needs* a good flabbergasting.

· · ·

CAPPED IN ICE and dusted with snow, the lake at Yihe Yuan had crystallized into a winter playground. Dozens of people crunched atop its surface, ambling amusedly across an area customarily beyond reach.

My first steps were timid, distrustful, but the others walked so calmly I had to join them. I ventured to the Stone Boat, where I'd picnicked with students in September, and patted its bow from a new vantage – lakeside.

The other ice walkers drew casual swoops and curves with their tracks. Nobody strayed far from the palace. I looked down the length of the lake, and the American in me kicked in. What fun was an ice bridge untraversed? In one shortcut to the lake's far end I could bisect the whole.

I turned my feet from my fellows and marched outward.

Yihe Yuan, September

Footprints quickly fell away until only an occasional line swept like a contrail across my path. I glanced back. The palace had shrunk already; the human figures beneath it were silent, tiny. That was how I appeared to them – a loner who'd stepped outside the community. I wondered if anyone noted my originality. Perhaps someone would follow?

The snow ahead lay untouched except for bird tracks. Then those, too, dropped behind. Utterly virgin, this half of the lake was all mine.

An odd patch lay ahead, a gray-blue discoloration perhaps a hundred yards away. Curious, I pushed forward. It looked like bald ice. Would I be able to slide, ice-skating fashion? I sped forward – then stopped dead in my tracks.

I was seeing water.

Water rippling in the wind. Fifty yards away.

How thin was the ice beneath me?

Fixed in fear, the nerves of my feet attuned to the slightest sensation. No creaking, no groaning. Safe for the moment.

How was it possible, open water in an otherwise frozen lake? A underwater vent, a heated pipe? With That Scene from *Never Cry Wolf* screaming in my head I dared the first steps backward, scrutinizing my footing, ready to grab at the ice should I crash through.

After a minute I rotated forward and permitted myself to breathe. The Summer Palace still presided over its carefree walkers, now just dark blips. I supposed signs posted in Chinese warned against straying too far – signs the illiterate Lao Wai had missed.

If I'd broken through, would anyone have seen me? Would anyone on the planet have had the faintest clue where to search for my body?

Yihe Yuan, January

I rejoined the other walkers, hoping no one would follow my footsteps. There was some wisdom in a crowd after all.

. . .

How are you doing that?" Johnny asked.

After our tutoring sessions he usually played my guitar. Hearing me now, though, his fingers froze over the strings.

I was reading aloud Chinese characters I'd never seen before. Effortlessly. Page after page.

"Oh, wow," Johnny said, setting down the guitar. "This is surprising me. I cannot figure how you do it."

The children's primer I was reading from introduced four characters on a page. Each appeared beneath a kiddie watercolor: duck, umbrella, car, dog, train, bowl, flag, rain – or, in later pages, soldier, tank, jet fighter, missile. Still, my Mandarin tutor reacted as though witnessing a miracle.

I pointed at the word 士兵. "Shi bing," I said.

Brow raised, Johnny asked, "You know what this means?"

"It's a soldier."

"Okay, *soldier* you know from the picture. But I do not believe how you say the words. You never have seen them?"

"Never. Pick any page, I'll read it to you." I was enjoying this. What Johnny wasn't noticing, though in plain black print, was the pinyin (phonetic spelling) beneath each character.

Imagine writing out a long number: thirty-three million, four hundred twenty-one thousand, eight hundred and nine. You could more easily write 33,421,809. If both forms appeared on a check made out to you, which would your eyes turn to first? One conveys instant meaning; the other requires decoding. Quick, what year is MCMXCIV – and how long does it take you to decode it? Johnny's failure to see the pinyin beneath each illustration paralleled our failure to read copyright years in Roman numerals.

After a few minutes of pretend magic I fessed up.

"I was really surprised," Johnny exhaled. "I could not think … wait, do it again." I continued reading pages of unfamiliar characters. Though he finally knew the secret, still he shook his head: "That is amazing me."

. . .

On a preposterously cold February morning I crept out of bed at five o'clock, sans breakfast, to meet friends arriving on an overnight train. Even at that hour the bus was standing room only.

As I planted my feet and gripped the overhead rail, a distinct boundary of numbness slid down my arm. Its frigid movement was methodical, distinct, like the slow line of water in a draining tub. Soon others lines joined in: from each hand and foot an icy band inched towards my torso.

I checked other passengers' expressions – could they see in my face a sign of what was happening to me? – and noticed a pulsing grayness clouding my eyes. The roar of the bus collapsed into a hollow whine, as if two Styrofoam cups were covering my ears, and I realized, "Oh, I'm passing out!" I hadn't been eating well. That, combined with the cold and early morning exhaustion, was shutting my body down.

My next thought: "No way am I going to pass out in front of all these people!" The Chinese weren't shy about staring. I wasn't about to give them the chance to mutter, "Hey, look at Lao Wai on the floor."

So I gripped the rail and resolved not to fall. Actually, falling may have been physically impossible considering how closely we were jammed together, but still: the more my vision blacked out, the more my hearing closed in, the tighter I clenched my fist around the rail. Within minutes I could see, hear, and feel nothing but the pitching floor. Then it, too, vanished, leaving me floating in womb-like darkness, simple and warm and free.

I discovered myself upright when the bus reached Xizhimen subway station, the end of the line. The twenty minute ride had taken only a few minutes, or so it seemed – apparently I'd lost my sense of time as well, along with every other conscious thought except the belief that, in some other world, a body that looked like mine was about to humiliate itself by crumpling to the floor, and I could prevent it through sheer willpower.

After staggering from the bus I sat on a curb for several minutes, then bought and slowly ate an egg and scallion pancake. I would be late to the railway station, but passing out again wouldn't get me there any faster.

As for not being gawked at, Lao Wai eating an egg pancake on the curb caught plenty of attention from passing commuters.

. . .

MY OUT-OF-TOWN FRIENDS INVITED ME to their own city, Taiyuan. We traveled back to the railway station to buy tickets, spent the day exploring downtown Beijing, and later returned to my apartment to fetch our luggage. After hearing so many zany stories about rail travel in China, I looked forward to my first experience.

Over dinner at a restaurant, however, I became ill. My stomach clogged; I visited the restroom twice. The skirmish in my guts only escalated. Vomiting? Diarrhea? Both seemed inevitable, yet here I was about to follow Nicole and Andrea to the railway station, to be locked in a swaying, smoky box with one restroom for fifty people – and that a porcelain hole in the floor.

Dinner progressed. I envisioned myself in a coach lavatory, hands braced against the lurching walls, alternately squatting for diarrhea or kneeling for vomit, a line of anxious people rattling the door for their turn. The force of sickness would cause me to miss the hole; the floor would become slippery; that, combined with the train's motion, would make me fall. No matter how I envisioned it, I couldn't think of a way to avoid being covered in my own filth.

Dinner ended. We were paying our bill when I cleared my throat and announced, "I don't think I should come. I'm getting awfully sick."

What? I didn't look sick.

"Didn't you see me leave for the restroom? Twice? It wasn't pretty."

Wouldn't it pass? I'd already bought my ticket!

"I'm pretty sure I'm going to end up vomiting. You really want to sit next to me for twelve hours?"

Somehow I convinced them I wasn't being silly. I wished them well at the bus stop, hoisted my bag and pedaled the ten minutes home, struggling not to foul myself.

I've done some traveling in my life, which is a polite way of saying I've endured some nasty digestive bugs. But that night – six hours of diarrhea and vomit coming so fast on one another's heels I didn't always have time to flush – that night ranked among the worst.

And the whole miserable time I thanked God, deeply, deeply thanked Him, for the foresight to stay off that train.

. . .

JOHNNY SOUNDED LIKE A PARENT with a toddler. "Zhe shi shen me (*What is this*)?" he asked, pointing at his nose.

"Bizi," I answered.

"Zhe shi shen me?"

"Erduo (*Ears*)."

For weeks I couldn't remember two words: *xiong* and *gebei*. Frustrated, I decided to brand them into my gray matter once and for all. I danced around my empty apartment like a ninny, thumping myself in my chest chanting "Xiong! Xiong! Xiong," then clapping my upper arms shouting "Gebei! Gebei! Gebei!" I gyrated wildly, switching between the two words in a crazed primeval chant.

They say it's impossible to tickle yourself. I suspect it's also impossible to embarrass yourself in front of only yourself ... but that night I got close.

Now, fifteen years later, I can't recall the Mandarin words for face, foot, or hand. But *xiong* and *gebei* are as clear to me as their English counterparts.

. . .

FOR CLOSE TO A THOUSAND YEARS the Chinese New Year arrived in Beijing to the rattling cacophony of firecrackers.

Then, silence.

On December 1, 1993, firecrackers became illegal in the capital of gunpowder's birthplace. Beijing residents spent the last few nights of November burning through the last of their pyrotechnics.

The idea was to prevent injuries; hospitals traditionally celebrated Spring Festival by treating burn victims. As *China Daily* explained, "In recent years, as people's standards of living improved, the custom of setting off firecrackers was taken somewhat to excess." The municipal government's solution was a blanket prohibition. "We believe that this action is an indication of a better and more scientific urban administration."

Firecrackers also had been used to celebrate weddings and to scare off demons at construction sites – occasions the government suggested would be served better by audio recordings.

Chinese New Year typically landed between late January and mid February. As it approached, I scoffed. Culture couldn't be thrown like a switch. The masses might comply, but a few brave souls would keep the spark alive. Beijing was big; they couldn't clamp down on *everyone*.

The clock ticked toward midnight. I listened for the crackling report of perseverance, rebellion.

Johnny's parents sharing their family photo album

Nothing.

Not one peep.

After an hour's watch I turned in for the night, a wiser man.

The first silent Chinese New Year in Beijing since gunpowder was invented: courtesy of the Communist Party.

. . .

COMPOSITION: WRITE A HOLIDAY STORY.

It happened just the night of New Year's Eve last year. Our New Year's Eve just like the West's Christmas. The family reunite and welcome the New Year's coming together. I had some business, so I was hold up in a small town. When I got the train ticket, it was nearly the Spring Festival. I had to spend two days on the train before I arrived at my hometown. So it was implied that I had to spend the night of New Year's Eve on the train. I felt very disappointed.

There were few passengers in the carriage. My opposite was a young man who wore a pair of glasses. I thought he must feel sad like me. Because he couldn't meet his family at the night of the New Year's Eve. Maybe his mother or his wife was waiting for his arriving. I couldn't think more because I almost cried.

In the period of the route, we talked little. We all maintained silent. The New Year's step was getting more and more closer. My heart was getting more and more heavier. The speakloud began broadcasting. A very graceful voice of girl spoke, "Good night, everyone. There left only half an hour to New Year. Let's welcome the New Year together." I raised my head and glared at him quickly. My face got red at once because he was looking at me. We maintained silent still. Although I wanted to say something to him, I didn't. The clock was beat at last. The New Year came. But I had not courage to say "Happy New Year." Time was passing. Two hours later, he began to pack his luggage. He would get off at the next station. The train pulled in. He stood up. While he went to the door, he seemed remember something and turned back. He gave me a paper, while smile, then went away.

I open the paper. There were three words on it. "Happy New Year." My tears welled up in my eyes.

. . .

ORAL EXAM COMPLETE, I stretched. Johnny tabulated.

"Maybe … four hundred words," he announced. Far short of our thou-

sand-word goal. He tried not to look disappointed in himself.

"Four hundred's a lot," I reassured. "And those others – I can almost remember them. My brain just needs time to sort them all out."

Johnny put on a positive face, but I could tell he wasn't persuaded. This was his first attempt at teaching, and he'd been more than enthusiastic. I wondered again about the Chinese capacity for memorizing. Surely my cranial retention paled next to his.

To be fair, I hadn't been operating at my prime – five weeks of wintry isolation had worn me down. During the fall semester my student Qian Da Liang had isolated himself in his dorm so he could spend all his time cramming vocabulary for the GRE. I hoped his spirits had fared better.

Four hundred words. Had I traded five weeks of traveling for coldness, flash cards, Chinese soap operas, meals alone, and a measly four hundred words? Suddenly the decision to winter in Beijing, "playing local," rotted. How much more I would have learned as a tourist! What kind of numbskull threw away five weeks of exploring such an immense country?

And I had disappointed my student-turned-teacher. "I'll keep working at it," I promised.

"No, you are right," Johnny said. "You are almost knowing a lot. It should be easy after this. And your accent is quite good I think. When you called last week, my wife can't know you are American. She thought you are another Chinese!"

"And you've gotten better at guitar," I said, nodding at the instrument in his hands.

"I don't have, so I have no way to practice. Sometimes I think you are paying me to learn guitar!"

"Well, you did an excellent job as a teacher," I said. "Thank you so much for spending all this time with me."

In five weeks I could have met a hundred people in two dozen cities. Instead I deepened a friendship with one. There was something in that.

Two days until the new semester. Teachers had begun reappearing around campus; students were refilling Da Shi Tang. After its long cold silence, Lin Da was stretching awake.

I looked forward to new students, to busyness, to the pressures and curveballs of teaching.

And I resolved not to miss a traveling opportunity again.

Street to Wudaokou :: Free Talk

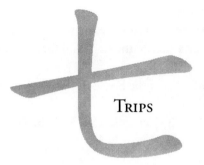

TRIPS

"Hong Kong was weird," fellow teachers reported upon their return. "Chinese people standing in line. We loved it, but it felt like *The Twilight Zone*."

The people we knew in Beijing did not stand in line. Not at the canteen, or the subway, or the bus stop, or the post office. Transactions were conducted through service windows, little holes that required bending down to speak through. I presumed any less of a barrier would permit people to crash right over the counter.

I used to think the elevator principle (Others Exit First) was self-evident. That was before I saw a group split by a subway rush. The doors opened, passengers tried to exit, the crowd pressed in, and two young men trapped inside were whisked from their friends.

Why all the pushing and shoving? Why would people who bicycled so calmly exhibit such impatience on two feet? I suspected the answer dealt with guanxi. The Chinese bound themselves powerfully to family, coworkers, friends; every kindness *had* to be reciprocated. Freighted by so much interpersonal debt, perhaps it was natural to skimp on courtesies to strangers. Some circles of humanity were inextricably tied to self; others were simply that: other. So why not sneak ahead? Everybody else was doing it, and in a culture that valued conformity that made cutting in line practically justified.

I actually found the moshing to be kind of fun, tapping as it did into childhood memories of the playground. Only once did a crowd make me fear for my safety. I was waiting at Xizhimen when an empty bus rolled forward and stopped with its door directly in front of me. I'd never seen an empty bus in Beijing; they were always so stuffed I'd never been able to sit down. People pressed at my back, squashing me against the shut door. Still, I smiled at the prospect of my first seat.

Then the door swung open and before I could lift a foot the crowd surged and I lost my footing. I missed the steps and for a second feared being trampled –

But no. I was lifted into the bus, completely in midair.

Did I get a seat?

Nope. By the time my feet connected with the floor, so many people had rushed around me the seats were filled.

. . .

MY NEW CROP OF STUDENTS persuaded me onto the soccer field. They were older than me, but not by much – and they wanted to see their American teacher in action because Americans were supposed to be strong. Americans were also notoriously ambivalent about the one sport worshipped by the rest of the world; perhaps they thought they could whup me.

There I stood, lone white guy on a Chinese soccer field at a Chinese university in Beijing, China, representing. Leading up to the game I feared humiliation. Thankfully years of service on high school soccer benches paid off, because I held my own.

Our game was rousing, spirited – and within five minutes I had to lean over, hands on my knees, at every break. Aside from bicycling I'd had zero exercise since arriving in Beijing. Ten aggressive minutes later I was ready to quit … but I was the teacher, the authority figure. If I stopped, they would stop. That's how their show of respect worked, and they were having so much fun I didn't want to ruin it.

So I kept playing. Enthusiasm was no trouble with all the rivalry and laughter, but my legs faltered, lungs burned. These guys played all the time; I was fading.

After thirty minutes I couldn't take any more. Let it be a lesson to them, I decided: not all Americans were strong. "I'm going to take a break," I said. "You keep playing, I'll keep score."

"No, we will stop." They called for the ball.

That dratted deference to authority! "No no no," I protested, "please keep playing. I just need to rest."

"We will rest too," they said.

Rats. "Alright then, I'll keep playing."

The game continued. Minutes dragged by; the ball seemed to quicken. So did they – I was having trouble making plays. Still, in such a lively game it was hard not to try, and I didn't like being shown up. They were so resilient! Let that be a lesson to me: the Chinese were healthier and tougher than I thought. This scrawny American couldn't even dash around a soccer field for an hour.

O! I was dying! At every break in the action I knelt on a knee. Surely any minute they would tire and stop. But no – they were still having fun. I struggled on for their sakes, as well as not to embarrass myself.

After an hour and a half I'd slumped into a zombie stupor.

"You all are so strong!" I protested. "I've got to stop. Please, you keep playing."

"We will stop too." They brought in the ball.

"No, please don't," I insisted, guilt-stricken. "I'd love to keep going but I can't, I'm so out of shape. Please, please keep playing."

"No, we will stop too," they said.

Nothing I could say would change their minds. We walked off the field bragging about each other's skills and clapping each other on the back. I don't know how my legs managed the four flights up to my apartment.

A week later, eating in Da Shi Tang with several of these students, I praised them: "I still can't believe how strong you are! My legs were sore for days."

"Mistah Hobison," they grimaced, shifting uncomfortably, "our legs are *still* sore."

That dratted deference to authority! They'd been bound to play as long as their teacher played.

With students at Yuanming Yuan (Old Summer Palace).
"The British burned it down in 1860," they told me – and glared.

"Hey, I'm not British," I said. They frowned. I was obviously splitting hairs.

123

. . .

PINK EYES BULGING from their downy white heads, the two rabbits hopped around Patty's apartment, sniffing everything.

"I still don't get why you bought them," I said.

"Well ..." Patty winced. "This man was selling them on the street, and when I asked how much they were he said three kuai (*bucks*) – per pound."

"Oh." So it was a rescue mission. "He was selling only two?"

"He had more. I couldn't see keeping more than two here." Idealism tempered by pragmatism.

Weeks later she brought the rabbits to my apartment. "I won't be able to bear saying goodbye to them at the end of the year, so I'm giving them to you."

"Just the rabbits? What about your fish?"

"Oh, you know – they're just fish."

Thus I owned pets in Beijing.

Accommodations were easy: my balcony served as a roomy hutch, and Wudaokou vendors sold plenty of fresh vegetables. My rabbits became an easy conversation piece during Free Talks, but I had to make a rule against lifting them by the ears – supposedly the proper way, except that they struggled and kicked as if in pain.

"What will you do with them when you go home?" students asked. I had no idea – prompting many offers to relieve me of my plump pets. "Yes, I will take good care of them," the men said, patting their bellies.

. . .

Rescued! Tie Dye and Disco

WHEN THE CHINESE PAUSED in mid-speech, thinking of what to say next, they didn't say *umm*. Instead they used one of two phrases: either *zhe shi* ("this is," as in "this is to say …") or *neige* ("that," as in "that word …").

My pursuit of a perfect Beijing accent demanded I drop the *umm*s – a difficult habit to break, but *zhe shi* sounded dignified enough to warrant the effort.

Students needed to make the reverse adjustment. Often their English sounded odd: "Yesterday I went to the, neige, the, neige, the grocery store and I bought some, neige, some vegetables. I bought tomatoes and carrots and … zhe shi, zhe shi … cucumbers." Technically this violated our English-only policy in class. Since most planned to study abroad, I didn't want them sounding like that.

Especially not *neige*.

"Never, ever say *neige* in America," I warned. "It sounds too close to a very bad word."

Their eyes lit up. "What is that word?"

I hesitated, then decided knowledge trumped innocence: they needed to know the word in order to avoid it. "I'm not going to say it – I'll just write it on the board.' Immediately I wished I'd warned them not to sound it out. "This word is very, very, very bad. It's the worst word in the English language. Never, ever say it."

"But you said *fuck* was the worst word."

Ouch – it was too easy to say curse words in a foreign tongue. I suddenly feared I'd taken the wrong approach – perhaps innocence trumped knowledge after all? Too late now. "You're right, I did say that, but I was wrong. This word's the worst."

"What does it mean?"

"It's a terrible, hurtful word for groups of people who started out in Africa." Oversimplified, yes, but the best I could come up with in the moment.

Thankfully it sufficed – they moved on. "But if we can't say *neige* or *zhe shi*," they complained, "what do we say?"

"Say what Americans say: *umm*."

They cracked up at the guttural noise. One dared, "That sounds … not intelligent."

"You're right," I admitted, "but that's what English speakers say, so that's our rule: no more *zhe shi* or *neige*."

We spent a minute practicing *umm*. It sounded all the dumber in a chorus of sixteen.

. . .

No ice cream in Beijing. No chocolate either.

Actually one *could* find chocolate, if one didn't mind masticating a waxy, tasteless wad that, like gum, refused to disintegrate. And one could find ice cream, if one's preferences favored the ice over the cream.

Standard Chinese treats were fruits, candied or taffied, tart enough to pucker your lips; and steamed buns, distant cousins to bagels, filled with a sweet, cinnamon-like bean paste.

In the winter, sidewalk vendors roasted yams atop coal-fired barrels. People ate them by peeling back the skin like a banana. Throughout the year, other street vendors boiled cauldrons of water to steam round racks of jiaozi and baozi (*buns filled with meat /vegetables*). Diners sat at folding tables and were served a few at a time, straight off the rack, until they'd had their fill.

. . .

Hannah had asked me to tutor one of her off-campus friends. I wasn't interested, so I declined politely – but then Hannah hoped I would find her friend a tutor. My fellow teachers were tapped out, and I knew practically no one in our area of Beijing. Unfortunately Hannah was using her guanxi with me to help her friend, making my wiggling out seem impossible.

One afternoon she called. I jotted down our conversation as soon as it ended.

> Hannah: Mistah Hobison, my friend found a tutor, but she (*incomprehensible*) and she wants you to (*incomprehensible*).
>
> Me: I'm sorry, what did you just say?
>
> H: My friend found an English tutor.
>
> M: Oh, okay – but you said something after that, what was it?
>
> H: I'm sorry, I can't hear you, there is too many people here and they are very loud.
>
> M: Okay. What was the last thing you said?
>
> H: There is too much noise here.
>
> M: No, before that.
>
> H: What?
>
> M: Earlier, right before that, about your friend.
>
> H: Before?
>
> M: Right.
>
> H: When? Yesterday?
>
> M: No, just now.

H: I'm sorry, I can't hear you.

M: I'm sorry, IS THIS BETTER? CAN YOU HEAR ME?

H: No, I mean I can't hear you – I *don't* mean I can't hear you, I can't understand you.

M: (*Huge sigh.*) So your friend found an English tutor.

H: Yes.

M: I'm glad to hear that.

. . .

AFTER MONTHS OF EYEING THEM WARILY, I took the plunge. I bought one of the eggs submerged in a vat of soy sauce.

My hesitation up to then came from a few unsavory experiences with thousand year eggs. But Da Shi Tang wasn't known for delicacies, so these brownish eggs made me curious. I'd never seen a student eat one up close.

Imagine my surprise when I removed the shell and found the inside white and yellow. It tasted normal, too, like a salted boiled egg – a fabulous addition to my diet.

The next day I paid for two. The server placed cracked eggs in my bowl – one slightly damaged, the other suffering a gaping crater. How long had it soaked that way in the vat? What color would *its* yolk be?

I flushed with anger. Merchants had passed off bad fruit, bad meat, a bad kettle on me because I was a naïve waiguoren. This time I wouldn't take it. I knew the score. I stayed at the window and told her, in my weak Mandarin, that I wouldn't accept the eggs.

Her response came so fast I couldn't follow a word, which made me even more stubborn. I stood my ground and repeated my measly phrase: "Bu yao, zhe ge huai le (*I don't want, this is broken*)." She got loud; a few students behind me got loud. In the echoing expanse of Da Shi Tang heads were turning.

In the end the server won: she had the vat of eggs, and she had my money. I slunk off to eat with my students.

"Mistah Hobison, the eggs are supposed to be cracked," one student informed me. "It lets in more soy sauce."

. . .

LIFE OVERSEAS wasn't all adventure. I spent most of the time preparing lessons and grading homework – a bit dull, to be honest.

This impression matched an experience I had in 1990 in Uganda. After days of initial thrills and challenges, a night came when I couldn't sleep and spent hours staring at a cracked plaster ceiling. There I lay on a continent I'd never imagined I would see, dead bored, fidgeting in bed, trapped in an existential plea: "Next moment, please?" It amazed me then, as it did in Beijing, that the exotic air I'd expected with every breath could leave me stuck in the solitary rattling of my own too-familiar thoughts. Consider this riveting entry from my journal:

> *Tues 5 Apr 94, Day 227: Taught, etc. Ate stuff, etc. Slept, etc. Mostly sleeping, depressed, exhausted, all that.*

Ten million people already lived in Beijing; the fact that I was doing so was nothing special.

By the second semester, little aggravations compounded to darken my outlook. A scowl at my attempted Mandarin, a pushy salesperson or a Lao Wai Special Price began to get the better of me. During this period my letters home dipped south of positive with some small-hearted overreactions – regrettable, but not unusual for that stage of culture shock.

More often people treated me with mere curiosity. And I encountered a few jewels who lifted my eyes beyond culture. People like Yang Jin Yu, the 65-year-old bicycle repairman who always threw an arm around me, tried fiercely to crack jokes across the language barrier, and insisted on fixing my bicycle for free. Or Hua Dongmei, the xia hai shopkeeper who taught me to use an abacus and gave me impromptu Mandarin tips. Johnny, who called one day to ask how I was doing simply because I'd seemed sad. Even the young boy on a late night bus who tried to cheer me with his limited English and infectious smile.

Yang Jin Yu kept me rolling in more ways than one

I wish I could tell them how such guanxi-free kindnesses boosted me. They were my lifelines.

. . .

I'VE NEVER ENJOYED HAIRCUTS: stabbing at conversation while a stranger fiddles with your head; missing the look you were hoping for, no matter how precisely you described it. Language obstacles made the process even less appealing.

The only barbers I saw worked along the main street outside campus, where they sheared draped men on stools. Fallen hair didn't need to be swept, it just blew away. Still, I balked at trapping myself on a stool in full view of gawking bicyclists.

So I didn't. I went eight months without a haircut, my thick curls growing straight up and out in a bushy Anglo Fro. I worried it would be seen as unprofessional, but students crowed, "It's The Explosion!" – the term, they explained, for the permed bouffant worn by some Chinese rock stars. That may not have qualified as professional, but at least it wasn't taken as ratty.

The situation changed when my mother confirmed she and a friend, Joan, would fly across the globe for a one-week visit. Playing international host for Mom dictated a haircut.

Out I tromped to the streetside barbers. A few hand sweeps and pinched fingers were enough to indicate what I wanted: total buzzcut. Zero chance for mistakes.

And none there were, until I showed up to teach in my fuzzy cue ball. Not only did it dismay my students (they'd enjoyed the rocker look), it unnerved them. "Are you *angry?*" they asked.

"No, why?"

"Why did you cut all your hair?" People shaved their heads as a political statement, they said – and they demanded to know mine.

"No, it's no statement," I explained, "I just needed a haircut." From beneath my shorn scalp, convincing them wasn't easy.

. . .

I LIVE JUST NORTH OF WASHINGTON, D.C., and you know how it is. I don't take nearly enough advantage. Monuments, federal buildings, Smithsonians … they're American, yes, but in a showy sense, disconnected from ordinary life.

So were Beijing's landmarks. I hadn't committed to an entire year overseas for some reconstructed swank – I wanted to experience China's unswept grit. Mostly I left the tourist traps alone.

Mom and Joan's visit, however, called for a sightseeing blowout. Each day, right after my morning classes, we dashed around like mad on public transport. In six afternoons we hit several hot spots:

Tiananmen Square. Some marble steps around the base of the People's Monument gleamed conspicuously brighter than others; rumor had it they'd been replaced after tanks rolled over them in 1989.

Forbidden City. We especially enjoyed the stone gardens – craggy, Swiss-cheesy boulders carted in from hundreds of miles away for their raw organic beauty.

Behai Park. A hilltop offered a spectacular view of the Forbidden City. We ate at Fangshan, where ¥100 per person brought out fourteen courses including sea slug and camel's paw.

Summer Palace. Willow trees, bridges, pagodas, and over 14,000 paintings of history and folklore decorating the Long Corridor, a covered walkway on the lake's north shore.

Great Wall. On every visit I had the same thought: "I'm on the Great Wall!" It never got old, nor easy – the wall climbed steep ascents along a mountain ridge.

Johnny brought us to a downtown restaurant for Peking Duck, a fancy name for what essentially were duck tacos. We balanced that with a taste of the everyday at Da Shi Tang, and by grocery shopping at Wudaokou, where I demonstrated my inept bargaining skills.

On top of all that, Mom and Joan attended many of my classes to present aspects of American culture and to serve as interview targets. A bad move, that: I should've expected that my students would ask a barrage of questions

Mom and Joan arrive

about me, which Mom answered with a slew of embarrassing stories.

. . .

AT THE FORBIDDEN CITY, Mom really had to go.

"There's a restroom right here," I pointed, walking her over.

"You don't have to come," she protested – but I wasn't being overprotective. She didn't know she needed a restroom ticket from a nearby booth. It wasn't expensive, just one mao, but still: paying to use a restroom was foreign to her.

"Now, when you get in there," I coached, handing her the ticket, "think baseball catcher."

"What? Why?"

"I'm not about to explain – you'll figure it out. Baseball catcher."

Puzzled, she entered the restroom.

She came right back out.

"What are you doing?" I asked. "You couldn't have –"

She intoned, "I don't have to go after all."

"But you were just saying how much you –"

She tugged me away. "I'll be fine, let's go!"

Public facilities were porcelain trays installed in the floor, one end slanting toward a drain. We Americans called them squatties. To be unduly frank, they opened up the bowels nicely, making a seated position seem inefficient and unclean.

Needless to say, I wasn't surprised when Mom emerged unrefreshed. Still, I had to rib her: "Look, Mom, I paid good money – get back in there!"

"No, that's quite all right," she pleaded.

Mom teaching

"Fine, then I'm getting my money back." I made a show of stomping to the ticket booth as if to request a refund – whereupon she buried her fingernails in my forearm and yanked me away.

. . .

I VIDEOTAPED ONE FREE TALK with Mom and Joan in attendance. Students looked into the lens and introduced themselves to our friends and family in America. Sally proclaimed her love for tennis and apples. Wanda explained that English was her path to a better secretarial job. "Zao gao (*Terrible*)!" classmates jeered when Matt had trouble finding his hometown on my wall map.

They treated us to "Wo Ai Beijing Tiananmen" with huge giggles, voices welling with enthusiasm. It was the first song they'd learned in grade school, trained by the Communist Party to love their nation. Afterward came the translation, delivered as a group effort. I didn't broach political topics with my students, so I was fascinated as their translation progressed on camera.

> GRACE: I love Beijing –
> MATT: I love Tiananmen Square. Yeah.
> WU LI YAN: Because Tiananmen Square –
> MATT: Because the sun, the sun rise above the square.
> GRACE: Every day, every morning the sun rise up from the Tiananmen Square.
> WU LI YAN: Tiananmen Square maybe is the one biggest in the world.
> GRACE: Our leader Chairman Mao lead us to go afroad – go forward.
> MATT: Yes, go forward.
> MATT: Chairman Mao give us guidance to advance forward.
> GRACE: And lead us from victory to another victory.
> WU LI YAN: All the Chinese people follow Chairman Mao. (*He raised his arm in a "go forward" gesture, tilted up and outward; everyone laughed with thumbs up.*)
> GERALD: Follow Mao Zedong thought.
> MATT: It is a song during the Mao Zedong period, time.
> SARAH: Yeah. Worship Chairman Mao.
> WU LI YAN: Yes.
> GRACE: The old people in old country always worshipped Chairman Mao, and sometimes think is, is just like a god. He leave us all

our sweet, our happy life, our sweet life.

ME: Xian zai zen me yang (*Now how are things*)?

GERALD: Cha bu duo le (*So-so; short of the mark but good enough*).

What this transcript fails to convey is their nervous laughter, eyes tracking each other's expressions. They weren't precisely *comfortable* divulging this much of their experience to waiguoren. Some voices flirted with sarcasm. Other tones sounded nostalgic, yearning wistfully for a time when the world was simple and magic was real.

"Well," I told Mom and Joan after they left, "you just saw in one evening more of the real Chinese mindset than I've seen all year."

. . .

WHAT DO YOU THINK?"

Mom kind of shrugged.

Minutes later I tried again. "Isn't it nice?"

Another noncommittal response, even a grimace.

"What, you're not impressed?"

I was showing off Lin Da's newly completed main building, a thirteen-story construct that towered over the six-story buildings on campus. A departure from the typical gray, its white finish virtually shimmered against the dull sky. A central column of black glossy windows rose toward a diamond-shaped flair at the top. As we walked halls of tiled walls and polished linoleum floors I was almost crooning, echoing university officials who'd given me the tour when I first arrived.

"Come on, admit it – this is way better than the other buildings."

Lin Da's newly opened main building

"Oh, sure," she said. "It's just not the best workmanship."

"What? What's wrong? Show me something not done well."

She pointed at a door handle: "It's just not top grade." The tiled walls: "See how quickly these were put up? The jagged seams?" The linoleum flooring: "Better than concrete, but most buildings in America wouldn't use something this quality."

"Mom, this is China! They don't have the kind of money America does."

"No, of course not," she said. "But I worry about you. You're just adapting to these standards so closely. You're *impressed* by this building." She said it as an accusation, then looked away. "I just wonder what's going to happen to you when you come back to the States."

. . .

I WAS EXHAUSTED. Teaching every morning and playing tour guide every afternoon and evening had drained me – by Day Four I was ready to collapse. Thankfully two students were begging to take Mom and Joan out on a girlie shopping spree.

This made me a little nervous. Release my mother to the big bad world of Beijing without me? I'd never been to their proposed destination, and was concerned about – oh, anything. But I needed a nap badly, and all four women kept repeating how much fun they would have and how fine they would be.

They returned in time for dinner after a fabulous outing. Mom had bought a Chairman Mao jacket and several small souvenirs. "But it was weird," she said. "Every time I put my bags down the girls were upset. They kept telling me not to put anything on the floor. Why is that? Is the floor

After the shopping spree

considered forbidden?"

"No," I said, "it's because people spit."

She winced, then blurted, "Oh, and we saw a fight."

"A *what?*"

"A fight. Two men going at it, right there on the street. Everyone rushed over so fast it was hard to see, and the girls were pulling us away."

A fight didn't compute. China was peaceable, group-oriented; nothing I'd experienced in eight months even hinted at the possibility of a fistfight. I shot off a dozen questions: who the fighters were, how it started, whether weapons were involved, if the crowd tried to stop them, if they were arrested. Above all: what could have inspired two men to shed all face and thrash each other in public?

"I'm sorry," Mom had to respond, "I don't know, the girls pulled us away immediately. They didn't want us to know about it at all."

Again, in just one week Mom had stumbled across an aspect of Chinese culture I hadn't experienced myself after months. I began to feel I could never understand this nation fully – it was simply impossible to plumb the individuality and uniqueness of a billion lives.

Which only made sense. After almost forty years my own nation continues to surprise me.

. . .

COMPOSITION: WHAT IS LIFE?

> I'm an atheist. Everything in the earth has its own origin, develop-
> ing road and end. Mankind can take advantage of nature and remold
> nature, but can't conquer nature. If we are against the law of nature,
> nature will punish us. The sun is heading into his middle age and finally
> it will die away. The earth also will meet its end. No one can change it.
> In addition, although we can predict something that will happen, there
> are so many things that happen unexpectedly. So mankind is the slave of
> nature and unexpectedness.
>
> Now our world is developing rapidly. With the help of science and
> technology, mankind has made great progress in meeting his need. That
> is people have made use of nature. But many problems have been devel-
> oped by or partially by mankind in the same time such as energy crisis,
> pollution, population explosion and food shortage. Many ways in the
> earth are radically related to these problems. Although people now come
> to realize the severity of these problems, it is certainly impossible to settle

them, I think. So people have been developing as well as destroying themselves.

Modern civilization create and provide very developed economy and advanced tools such as plane and telegram. But people always feel tension and constraint. In the big cities, people work hard to earn money for housing and other necessities. People look for job, look for promotion, struggle and survive. Sometimes, I think it is nonsense that people struggle and survive and then die. Human beings are something of material. And they will extinct in the future.

. . .

LAO JIA (*EXCUSE ME*)," coughed a man's voice. From the top bunk I looked at a middle-aged gentleman in a business suit. Ticket in hand, he gestured at my bunk and spoke beyond my comprehension.

An hour earlier I'd hugged Mom and Joan at the airport for their flight home, then jumped into a taxi and headed to the rail station for some traveling of my own. I'd just spent a week flaunting my navigation skills; now it was time to put them to the test in my first trip to another city. Sure enough, even before the train set out I'd goofed. I was in the wrong seat.

But when we compared tickets, the businessman discovered he'd read his wrong. Score one for the waiguoren – maybe he wasn't a *complete* idiot.

Rail travel earned its rough reputation. In such a large nation, even a city as close as Taiyuan took twelve hours to reach. Most people, including foreign teachers on shoestring budgets, rode hard seat, the equivalent of an unpadded city bus seat that left overnight travelers to catch whatever sleep

Steam engines were still in use

possible from an upright position. A plush upgrade to soft seat was available, but since this was my first rail trip in China I opted to pamper myself with a bunk. The choice then, hard sleeper or soft, was no choice at all – my Taiyuan friends would chide me if I wimped out entirely.

Hard sleeper it was: a passenger car divided into about a dozen open sections of six firm bunks each, three on a side. Picture an infantry car and you've got it.

As the train started off, men sat at the no-smoking signs beside the windows to smoke. Two couples played cards on the bunks beneath me and discussed whether or not I could understand them. In the bunk across from me a preteen boy fiddled with a Walkman and snuck glances at the funny-looking Lao Wai.

The train stopped regularly at small towns. I paced the car often, other passengers eyeing me. A college woman asked if I was Middle Eastern; she was studying Arabic at Bei Da (*Beijing University*). When I told her where I worked, a whispered grapevine of "Linye Daxue" ran both directions along the car.

The lights cut off at 10:30PM. Cigarettes went out; windows went up, trapping the muggy air. Conversations hushed, leaving us rolling to the soft chorus of seventy-odd bodies in deep-breathing sleep. The rhythmic clacking of rails joined exhalations all around like a gentle rain. Despite this lullaby, I woke throughout the night with the train's frequent stops.

6:30AM: lights on. People read Communist newspapers; the men smoked Communist cigarettes.

By midmorning we reached Taiyuan, famous city of vinegar. I'd hoped for Exotic and New, only to be disappointed by the dingy sameness Taiyuan shared with Beijing. Dust. Smog. Buildings the color of bus exhaust.

My friends Nicole and Christine K. met me at the station. "Everyone's staring," I said stupidly. Yes, people stared at waiguoren; I knew this. But in Taiyuan eyeballs *lingered*. Unnervingly.

"Oh, that's right," Nicole laughed, "you've been in Beijing this whole time – they're used to foreigners. Welcome to Taiyuan! There's just twenty or thirty of us in the whole city."

"Just be glad you don't have blonde or red hair," Christine K. added, "like us."

. . .

SHOULDER TO SHOULDER, CHEST TO BACK, people got pressed on buses. It was the nature of mass transit: firm physical contact with all contiguous bodies.

Still, what was up with *this* woman?

Nicole and Christine K. were taking me by bus to their campus. They'd managed to snag seats a few rows back; I stood in the stairwell, two steps down, back to the wall. And this woman …

No cultural difference may be more jarring than the degree to which others approach and touch your own body. In China guys leaned on each other's shoulders or wrapped arms around a male friend's neck. In a crowd, people possessed about the same personal space as a litter of puppies.

This woman, though. She'd shoved against me so hard I'd pulled back against the wall, trying to squeeze out of her way, and still she was shoving. Now that I was cornered it seemed her body was becoming more intent, and as the bus jounced us down the street she swayed into me, turned away so I couldn't see her face but tilting her hips back, pressing into me, rubbing, grinding …

Call me slow. Eventually I realized she expected a physical response – and, presumably, a financial one.

Hadn't she noticed my friends? Did she expect me to abandon them with a cheery "Catch up with you ladies later – I'm heading off with this hussy"?

Blushing deeply, I looked back for help. Nicole and Christine K. could barely see me, much less the nuance of this sub-waist offensive. At the next stop I twisted out of the stairwell and pushed through other passengers to stand closer to my friends.

We resumed our prior conversation, but my mind reeled. Obviously the woman had targeted me because I was a waiguoren, away from the accountability of my home network. Was she a hooker? From movies I expected glitzy heels and too much lipstick on a street corner, but in April everyone still bundled up in coats. Did prostitutes regularly work the buses undercover? Suppose I'd taken the bait – would she have brought me to a hotel, a brothel, her apartment? Had anyone else realized she was propositioning me? She didn't seem to move to other men after my escape, but then it was difficult to tell, it had all been so subtle.

Keeping silent about such a bizarre incident made me feel two-faced in front of my friends, but I couldn't quite shake the feeling of humiliation.

. . .

I'D NEVER DONE ANYTHING like it. I was nervous. Wasn't Chad nervous?

"Not really," he said. "I've been through most of those areas before. The only thing to be concerned about is the wild dogs. And that was just once."

Chad – four years older, thirty pounds stockier, with a shock of coarse sandy hair and a Schwarzenegger jaw – looked like he could handle wild dogs. "What'd you do?" I asked.

"Well, we couldn't outrun them on bike," he said, "not on a gravel road with all our gear. So we pelted them with rocks 'til they ran off."

I imagined the scene: two waiguoren on mountain bikes pedaling an unpaved road through a sea of grassy slopes in the middle of nowhere China. No people, no trucks, just a mischievous pack of dogs hounding them. *Call of the Wild*, without the guns or whips.

"I don't know," I said.

"Look, Chris is gonna come." Chris was a friend from our Los Angeles training; I'd met Chad only the day before, there in Taiyuan. "If she can do it, you can."

Other people crossed vast areas by bicycle – people in magazines. Not me. I could count on one hand the number of times I'd gone camping.

But that also lured me.

Five weeks. Western China. Areas that spoke different dialects of Chinese, or even different languages altogether. Muslim groups, Buddhist groups, right in the middle of an atheist regime. To see it all by bike would be the adventure of a lifetime. How could I say no?

I would need a mountain bike, saddlebags, a sleeping bag. Since I lived in Beijing, I would also hunt down and buy us a tent.

I would also need to exercise like crazy. We would bike eight to ten hours a day: four or five in the morning, afternoon xiuxi (*rest*), four or five before dark. To my recollection I'd never ridden a bike over two hours, and that was without camping gear.

Chris was going. She and Chad were dating, and they wanted a third person as a chaperone, a sort of anti-hanky panky measure. Otherwise, no trip. Wouldn't I go?

Up to that point I'd seen only brown Beijing and even browner Taiyuan. Would they be the only impressions I carried back to America?

Nine hundred miles away a pack of wild dogs whined for me. Rocks didn't seem much of a solution; in fact I had no solution at all, no idea what I'd do given that scenario, not to mention countless others unforeseen. And there was something thrilling in that, in committing to risks I had no idea how to handle.

I was in.

. . .

BACK IN BEIJING I was maneuvering through the railway station when a scruffy four-year-old with a runny nose walked up, said something and extended a hand. She held three mao.

"No thanks, bu yao," I answered, wondering why a child would offer me money. Then I realized she was singing a song – a begging song. Mussed hair, grimy teeth, cheeks caked in dust: an orphan? I thought Communism provided for people.

No one else in the station seemed concerned about her plight; perhaps they realized something I didn't. I walked on and saw her dash away to rejoin her mother – her fairly clean, fairly well-dressed mother.

Panhandling strategy notwithstanding, how could a mother keep her own child in squalor?

On the bus ride home I watched a welcome contrast, a father lifting his six-month-old son to the handrail, letting him grab with his tiny hands, then lowering him until he could almost support his own weight. Up, down, up, down, for no other reason than to delight his boy. Yes, the Chinese loved their children. The woman at the railway station was an anomaly. I wondered about the circumstances that had driven her to such a dire measure.

In the middle of this reverie someone brushed into me. Bodies bumped all around, but this was different.

Close contact prompted most waiguoren to keep their money and ID in a waist pack – a wise policy in this case, as the brushing persisted. Moments later it resumed from behind: an alternating tapping, light enough to seem imagined.

At the next stop bodies shifted, and I squeezed to the other end of the bus (no small feat). But I felt the sensation again, rhythmic, insistent yet faint. No one around me looked suspicious. I'd wrapped my coat in my arms, covering the waist pack, and when I next felt the fanning it included the unmistakable intrusion of flesh – four fingers jiggling their way toward my belly, where they encountered my hand.

The fingers jerked back and I wrenched around to see who was behind me. A short, dark-complected man with a tight crew cut studied the windows. I recognized him from the other side of the bus – he'd been one person away from me in the crowd, and had followed me all the way to this side determined to score.

Preservation of face required a facade of peace. I knew this. My pickpocket knew it too, and thrived on it.

But I wasn't Chinese. I was American, and had already given him an easy out by moving away. Time to handle it my way.

I faced him square on and asked in a booming voice, "Ni yao shen me

(*What do you want*)?"

Everyone heard; everyone looked. The man stood rigid, glowering. He refused to meet my eyes.

"Ni yao shen me?" I demanded, again loud enough for all to hear. I swelled with anger. Was he poor? Did he have a family to feed? Such possibilities didn't occur to me. I knew only that he'd targeted me because I was a waiguoren, on the heels of others targeting me because I was a waiguoren. I was sick of it.

He remained there, burnt red, wishing himself out the window, one arm raised to hold the ceiling handrail. I tapped his fingers up there and spat, "Nide zhe ge tai man le (*Your this is too slow*)." Poor Lao Wai, who couldn't remember the word for *hand!*

Then …

Then it was awkward. I'd made a scene, causing everyone to watch us. I wasn't about to hit him or anything, and he wasn't about to make a single move acknowledging what had just occurred. Still everyone watched. No one spoke to the man, as I hoped they might, nor to me. Having scolded to the limits of my vocabulary, I'd said my piece and was finished. Pressed together on the bus, there was no escaping for either of us; we had to continue side by side in the fishbowl of attention I'd created. I wondered if the bus driver had heard, wondered if authorities would get involved, wondered what the consequences might be for a pickpocket.

Finally the bus stopped, the man twisted through to the exit, and I managed to exhale. It was over.

Apartment view :: Rice paddy northwest of Beijing

Spring

At long last, trees budded with a whisper of green so slight it seemed a hoax. Spring had arrived weeks earlier in name than in life, an agonizing tease.

Two days later branches erupted with confidence – the sweetest, warmest green I'd ever seen. I couldn't stop gazing at them. After the long gray winter my eyes were parched, desperate to drink in color.

. . .

I WASN'T GOING TO CYCLE across western China on my classical upright. I needed a mountain bike.

Diamondback manufactured in China and maintained an outlet in Beijing. I asked a student to accompany me as translator. After a year of seeing only single-gear bicycles on the streets, I felt like we'd entered a Ferrari dealership. So did Nate, a thirty-year-old businessman who took on a fatherly role: "We must go. These are not good, they are too expensive. I will find you another shop."

But I was scared enough of the upcoming trip that I wanted something lightweight, robust, and expensive. I settled on a midrange model with Shimano gearshifters and brakes: ¥3,300. Three months' salary for me, twice that for a Beijinger.

"I do not think this is a good idea," Nate kept protesting. "We should come back another day."

I needed to start training immediately, so for this purchase I forced myself into the mindset of American currency. We jaunted to the bank, changed $400 of my emergency cash, and made the purchase, Nate sweating the entire way.

"Please don't tell the class how much it cost," I begged on our ride home. I didn't want to seem like a spoiled American – I was only trying to buy survival.

Half an hour back at my apartment, I heard the knock: a dozen students who'd heard already and wanted to see. Nate had kept the Diamondback's cost a secret, but they clearly recognized its worth.

That made me nervous. I wouldn't be able to park it in public, not even with the ponderous chain I'd bought – it was too hot. So I uglified the frame by wrapping it in duct tape to give it a flat, grid-gray finish, and I brought it out of my apartment for distance training only. Otherwise I continued riding my grandfatherly clunker.

. . .

THE AUDIENCE BUZZED. "This man," my student Tony gushed, pointing in the program at what I took for a name, "is erhu genius. Perhaps he is the best erhu player in China."

"Really." We were sitting on wobbly folding chairs in Da Shi Tang.

"Yes. Some years ago there was a famous movie about erhu. This man recorded all of the music for the movie."

"Wow." Then what was he doing at Lin Da? Tables had been pushed aside to pack in extra seats before a makeshift stage. Still illiterate, all I knew about this concert came from posters around campus: date, time, and the image of an erhu.

Classical Chinese music enchanted me, especially the erhu. Most radio

*Duct tape
and water*

stations mirrored our styles: pop, rock, even rap (but no country, making country music a fantastic salve for homesickness). But unlike American radio, classical Chinese music got decent air time. The erhu's plaintive resonance haunted me into buying cassette after cassette.

The instrument itself was similar in concept to the violin but looked entirely non-Western: two strings suspended by a thin pole above a small wooden drum. Like the violin it lacked frets; unlike the violin it lacked a neck to press the strings against. Bending the strings, performers delved into wistful solos that wormed inside me, echoing my yearnings for home.

There in the darkened cinder block canteen of a little university on the northern edge of Beijing, Tony was telling me I was about to witness an erhu genius. "He is best in China, so I think he must be best in the world."

"I'll bet," I said.

But then Zhou Yaokun took the stage, and he was.

Four instrumentalists accompanied him, including a flutist and a man playing a relative of the accordion. Their music vibrated with energy, polish, inspiration – and in solo after solo, Zhou brought forth sounds impossible from a can, stick and two strings.

Had such music ever filled so lowly a setting? Probably not, which energized the audience all the more, applauding as if in answer to miracles.

Unfortunately, every time Zhou broke into innovation – super-quick plucking, percussive drumming on the strings, fingers unleashing unorthodox sounds I have no hope of describing – the audience clapped immediately, drowning it out.

"No, what are you doing!" I wanted to shout. Tantalized by brilliance I'd never heard, feared I might never hear again, I could catch only brief snatches before clapping thundered it away. We kept still for the butterfly's approach,

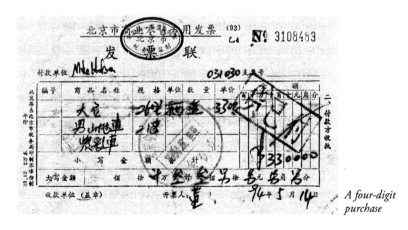

*A four-digit
purchase*

only to jolt every moment it alighted. The stony silence of American audiences must seem unaffected in comparison, but still ...

After the concert Tony ushered me to the stage. I was a nobody, an unachieving American kid fresh out of college, yet Tony insisted I shake hands with the world's top erhu player. Desperate for some memento of the evening, humility didn't stop me from requesting Zhou Yaokun's autograph, which he kindly supplied on the only piece of paper I had.

. . .

COMPOSITION: WHAT IS LIFE?

> *I think that one person, whoever is good-looking or ugly, rich or poor, perfect or disabled, if only he (she) has been on the earth, he (she) should own some human rights without deprivation. Such as the living right, the liberty of conscience and the right of pursue happiness. So everyone should live with his own lifeway, not imitate others or interfere others. In short, if all crippled person in China could ride wheelchairs and play game with others, our country would become equal, free, and rich.*

. . .

CHAD AND CHRIS DELEGATED tent procurement to me, which made sense – if a tent could be found anywhere, it would be in Beijing. Little did we suspect our miscalculation: the Chinese didn't camp.

In fact camping seemed rather antithetical to the Chinese mindset. What Americans view as an adversary to be tamed they regarded as a fickle behemoth best dealt with through negotiated coexistence. Rather than cut through woods or conquer mountains, they strolled in gardens on paved paths with flags, potted flowers, and loudspeakers issuing gentle reminders (no littering).

Zhou Yaokun's autograph

Why fight nature? It would always win, whether through storm, flood, drought, earthquake, or any of its other uncivilized whims. Better to tease out and mold its ways into a comfortable experience, crafting a stable guanxi between people and environs. They landscaped parks with an elemental balance of water, rock, plants and architecture – three parts nature, one part us.

Sleeping in a nylon dome in the middle of an untamed landscape? Not exactly their vision of a vacation. Hence, no tents. Not at Wudaokou market, not in the midtown shopping district, not even in the largest downtown department store I could find. From the odd looks salespeople gave me, I wondered if the word I'd looked up in the dictionary referred only to military shelter.

American tents must have been manufactured in China. Were they *all* shipped overseas – every last one?

Finally my student Leon accompanied me to a new megamall, a multi-level whopper straight out of Tokyo or Hong Kong that made Wudaokou look positively backwater. There, in an L.L. Beanish store, down an aisle in the back, on a bottom shelf where they appeared more forgotten than displayed, we found two 6'×6' tents.

Leon estimated the size with his arms. "I think it is too small for three people."

With no alternatives, size wasn't an issue. Neither was the ¥340 sticker. I paid and carried home fifty percent of Beijing's tent supply.

. . .

COMPOSITION: WHAT IS LIFE?

> *Chinese young men (and young women) have vigor. We have deep love for nature, for life. We often walk in the country to enjoy nature's flavors, to release ourselves from the monotonous and depressing life. Only in nature, we just feel the charm of life, the beauty of the earth. Only in nature, we just extricate from the noise of this mortal world, which is full of falseness, greed, prejudice and vanity. Sometimes we feel sorrow. Sometimes we feel hopeless. And sometimes we feel that we don't dominate ourselves. So we hope to go to a free kingdom (realm of freedom). I don't think it is an escape, because one person's life is limited. We are not willing to spend our life on an infinited waitness. We have no alternative.*

. . .

EVEN WITH THE DIAMONDBACK I was scared. In two months I would bisect western China powered by nothing but my own two legs. I had no idea if I could keep up, and no idea what would happen if I couldn't.

I needed to train. Ferociously. Fear of lying abandoned next to a far-flung mountain range goaded me.

The first Saturday after buying the Diamondback I loaded my water bottles and stuffed my waist pack with dehydrated fruit and fried soy beans. A few days earlier I'd bought a terrain map of the region. One road shot north from Yihe Yuan – I would follow it and climb into the mountains.

I raced freely on the early morning streets, indulging the itch for speed I'd felt all year, a Corvette among Pintos. Although I'd left at 6AM to avoid traffic and heat, by the time I reached Yihe Yuan and turned north the roads already swarmed with taxis, trucks, and slow-coasting bicycles. The route I'd selected turned out to be a sculpted avenue: canal to the left, sunlight glinting through flashing leaves above. As I sprinted, an army truck packed with young soldiers began to pass. "Kuai, kuai (*Hurry, hurry*)!" they laughed, waving me on. I worked the pedals madly to keep up. Further north the traffic cleared and the truck pulled ahead, leaving me racing for the sheer joy of movement.

Trees fell behind; so did the canal. Under the full sun I cranked across a gravel road cutting across a withered field. Heat radiated from the loose gravel beneath my tires. The mountains seemed just *there*, tauntingly close, but I'd outdone myself with the earlier sprinting. Now I crunched across the gravel coals modestly, dutifully, intent on the mountains ahead.

Suddenly something was different.

My face had turned leather. My skin felt like a mask wrapped around my skull, cooking my flushed head when it needed to breathe. I'd stopped sweating. Dehydrated? I guzzled my last bottle of water, hoping to resume sweating. It didn't work. Something was wrong, something was wrong –

So close ...

148

some core switch in me had flipped, shifting my body to a different mode, and there in the direct sun, not sweating, my face thick and hot, I turned my bike against the mountains with one thought: water.

I'd left canal, shade and civilization twenty minutes earlier. Needing to escape the relentless sun, I pedaled slower, trying not to heat myself further, appreciating even the mild movement of air. The skin of my face had died. I pawed at it, pinching my cheeks. Arms too, and legs, chest. I wasn't sweating anywhere.

Back at the tree-lined avenue I bought a liter of water and downed it. Then I sat near my bike, cooking in my flesh as people gawked. Did I look *that* odd? Or were they just staring at Lao Wai with the expensive bike?

Minutes passed; no sweat. I bought another liter, drank as much as my stomach could hold. Still no sweat. My gut bloated with water, yet the rest of my body roasted like a dry Crock-Pot. Wrong wrong wrong.

Sluggish, thoughts cloudy. What was happening? Still an hour from home. Get back. Bought more water, strapped it on, headed south.

I don't remember much about that return trip. In retrospect I should have hired a cab, but I wasn't thinking clearly. I do remember repeating to myself, "Just get home, just get home," and I remember having trouble staying upright. I drank more water but failed to resume sweating. People stared as they rolled past, easily outpacing me now as I focused on balance and pedaling. What were they seeing to make them stare? Was I that wobbly?

It must have taken two hours at that pace, but somehow, finally, Lin Da rolled into sight. I stopped at a xia hai store to buy a tub of sherbet, then at my building faced a final challenge: four flights of stairs. No way would I lock the Diamondback outside. Bleary, dizzy, I hoisted it onto my shoulder and concentrated on one step at a time.

Fellow teachers Patty and Melissa met me on their way down. "What's wrong with you?" they asked. Later they reported that whatever I said was indecipherable. Inside my apartment I downed the full pint of sherbet and collapsed in bed, not to wake again for sixteen hours.

Thankfully, after all that sleep I was fine.

Years later I took a wilderness first aid course and learned about heat stroke. The instructor confirmed that my experience matched the symptoms perfectly.

"I guess I was lucky," I said. "I was in another country, I didn't know a thing about the medical system, but it turned out okay."

"You're more than lucky," she said. "Fifty percent of heat strokes end in death."

. . .

4:45AM – HEAD OUT. Bike loaded with one-liter water bottles, hand-size bottles; backpack stuffed with bananas, beans, tools, spare tubes.

6:00AM – Rest on the far side of the closest mountain range, in a wooded cove near a quiet intersection. Eat bananas, beans. Refill smaller bottles from the liters.

7:30AM – Return to Lin Da. Shower, dress.

8:00AM – Arrive at Foreign Language Building to teach.

That training period stands out as one of my life's peaks. The dreary winter and the routine of teaching had dragged me into a rut, but suddenly I was waking earlier than just about everyone else in Beijing and circling mountains. I swept through areas most Beijingers never saw: river-scrawled valleys. Bridges, farmland, small villages. Desolate factories.

Was I *permitted* to bike anywhere I wanted? From what I could tell, most Chinese didn't just up and explore. I'd even heard some areas were closed to waiguoren. At one point the road flirted with a barbed wire fence and military-looking signs. Suppose this was a weapons plant, a nuclear facility – could I be questioned as a spy?

After pedaling 75 minutes out from pitch dark to budding sunrise, I would rest each day in the same secluded cove, trees shielding me from view in the unlikely event of a passing truck. Did this undesignated intersection of sleepy mountain roads have a name? Utterly detached from Lin Da, my whereabouts unknown to any other, I might as well have been on the moon.

The irresponsibility of it made me giddy. Already exhausted, it would take all my strength to get back in time to teach. A flat tire would make me

Along the early route

late; a bike-wrecking spill would make me miss my first class altogether.

The vast outdoors, the sense of breaking out, the element of risk – all so gloriously invigorating.

ONE OF THE STORES at Wudaokou began piping Nintendo music into the street, presumably to attract customers. I'd never noted the place but was surprised that it sold video games.

One day curiosity prompted me to peek in. Racks and racks of women's clothing – not a single video game anywhere.

Go figure.

. . .

WHERE TO FIND A BAG big enough to carry a bike?

Over the course of the trip we would take several train rides. I could pay to store my Diamondback on a baggage car but feared my poor language skills wouldn't be able to manage the arrangements. Besides, I didn't like the idea of my expensive bike being away from me for an extended period. Was it easy to steal from a baggage car?

Instead I resolved to break the Diamondback down into components and slide them under my bunk. How I would avoid alerting the conductor would come down to a combination of smiles and sneakiness – a fun challenge.

But first I needed a bag. A big one.

None of my students had ever heard of such a bag. Come to think of it, neither had I.

"This is how small I can make it," I showed them, dismantling the bike into pedals, wheels, frame and handlebars, then piling them into a bundle. Their faces darkened. Still, they told me they would find out.

A few days later Nate asked me to bring the Diamondback to Wudaokou. Riding it openly through the market felt odd – I'd never seen such a bike in public and didn't want anyone tracing mine back to my apartment (considering the sui bian security of my building, I kept it locked to my dining table, just in case). We rolled behind the vendors to a series of open-faced manufacturing shops, one filled with industrial sewing machines.

Nate introduced me to a worker who appraised the size of my bike. He was shaking his head. "Wait," I said, digging out my tools. I broke down the bike and packed it as tight as I could, then sketched out my vision for how a carry bag would be constructed.

We discussed the idea for several minutes, Nate interpreting my suggestions as well as the worker's experienced objections. Finally the man smiled, wiped his forehead and laughed – at me, at my drawings, and most of all at himself. He'd do it. And despite my willingness to pay him whatever he asked, he'd do it for free, simply because it was so bizarre.

I'd expected to use canvas, but the worker unrolled a stretch of thick plastic weave with red, white and blue stripes, the kind used to shield construction sites from view. It would be lightweight, waterproof, and just as strong. Then he modified my sketch, producing a simple folded design with grommets along the top to tie the bag closed and two straps to sling it over my shoulder. He asked me to return in a week.

A week later there it was, just as we'd envisioned: a flattish taco sewn on the sides, three and a half feet long, two feet high, with a craftsmanship tougher and surer than I'd hoped. He bragged about the triple-stitching he'd used, the thickness of the threading, the sturdiness of the grommets and the strap.

Of course he would accept no money. Instead he would enjoy telling the story of the crazy American who wanted a purse big enough for a bike.

. . .

BETWEEN CLASSES ONE MORNING, Henry informed me that laughing out loud was immoral.

"What?" I was suddenly self-conscious. Had I just been … ? How often did I … ? "Wait, are you sure?"

"Yes. If no one else is laughing, it is immoral."

"Do you really mean *immoral?*" I pressed.

"Oh," he said. "Maybe I'm using the word incorrectly."

In the classroom

. . .

OVER TWO SATURDAYS I built up endurance through extended forays north: two hours out, then two and a half. Determined not to repeat the heat stroke, I paced myself and carried a ludicrous amount of water.

The third Saturday I would pedal to the Great Wall.

I could see it dangling up there on the map. Students had mentioned that the Olympic cycling team biked the highway route to the Great Wall regularly, so it was doable. Rather than aim for Badaling or Mutianyu, I targeted an area where a pencil-line road snaked up and intersected the wall without a label – a section unrestored, without security guards to curb my exploration. Four and a half hours out, I estimated, and four and a half back. It would be a long day, but I needed to accustom myself to long days. Out I went.

After I reached my prior record of two and a half hours north, the road began a murderous mountain ascent. I spent the better part of an hour grinding up turn after turn, unable to see how high the road would climb, hoping for a tunnel to cut through. It was hot and my bike dragged with three liters of water, but I spurred myself with the knowledge that as soon as I rounded the top I'd see the Great Wall in the distance.

Dripping with sweat, I rounded one curve and braked to a stop. Ahead stretched a cartoonish darkness, a gaping maw thirty feet round, punctuated by the smallest pinpoint of light. A Road Runner tunnel, impossibly become real.

It *looked* safe. No trucks had passed for a while. Apart from the drone of insects, everything was still.

Sunlight illuminated a short distance beyond the jagged rim. Beyond

Tunnel and the road below

that, nothing. My eyes would adjust, I assured myself – but would an approaching truck see me? I scanned the switchbacks beneath me: no trucks, but that was only one side of the tunnel. The quicker I sped through, the better.

Clenching my teeth, I accelerated into the gulf of damp air. As the light behind me diminished, the piercing star ahead prevented my eyes from adjusting, making the darkness even more impregnable. I hadn't counted on that. I sped on, chilled blackness wisping away my heat.

The light wasn't getting larger.

Anxious about trucks from behind, I turned my head, and in the total absence of peripheral cues began to veer. I jerked back. How close had I come to the rocky wall – two feet or two inches?

It struck me too late that this was the act of an utter fool. At my speed, a single stone or pothole would spill me across the asphalt, wrecking my bike. Rats surely skulked in the darkness; any moment I would strike one. Or worse, a gang of highwaymen could be crouching along the walls, chains and planks ready to knock me flat. Terrors swept my skin as I raced through the black hollow.

The light wasn't getting larger.

Or was it? Frozen forward, my eyes inhaled the pinhole light. I pedaled frantically, crazed by the thought that others were watching my approach with dark-adjusted eyes. A cold slipstream hissed across my ears, masking all other noises. There was no asphalt below, no rock above, only the single point ahead and the weightless dark of space through which I hurtled.

Finally the exit grew into a bright disc, then a wider diffusion of warmth. The road rematerialized beneath me. I emerged. Rather than exploding around me, the sunlight touched down gracefully, like the relaxed whir of insects along the open road.

My shirt, drenched in condensation, began to warm in the sun. The road had been smooth. No one had accosted me.

On the way home I would have to pass through the tunnel again. Glancing back through the darkness at the small bright point where I'd started, I shivered.

And then smiled.

. . .

AHEAD LAY RIDGE UPON RIDGE, a veritable sea of rocky waves. I scrutinized each, trying to discern the faint curve and intermittent boxes of the Great Wall. Nothing. Wherever it was, it wasn't visible from here.

The road immediately plunged in steep switchbacks. I winced through each, knowing I would need to huff back up later.

Near the bottom a valley opened. I could see my road leading down, where it leveled and then crossed another road curling in from an adjacent valley. Beside this intersection perched a guard station with four police officers.

It was precisely what I'd feared in all my excursions: blundering into a forbidden area. I hadn't seen a single vehicle on my road in half an hour. The intersecting road was equally quiet, giving the four officers nothing to do but watch me approach. I could just hear their thoughts: "Bicycle coming down the mountain. Don't see that often. Yup, a bicycle, coming right this way. Fellow doesn't look very Chinese. Well ... he'll be here soon enough. Definitely not Chinese. This should be interesting."

With nowhere to hide, I began waving from a few hundred yards up and kept at it every few seconds, broadcasting a smile I hoped they could see the whole way.

When I rolled up they surrounded me, curious and cordial. They checked my ID, copied down where I worked, asked where I was going.

"Dao Chang Cheng (*I'm going to the Great Wall*)," I responded. They guffawed. Two men stepped around to take in my water-laden steed from different angles.

"Wo men zai nar (*Where are we*)?" I asked, pointing at my map. This intersection didn't appear, but from how long I'd biked I guessed the Great Wall lay across the next mountain. Their fingers landed on the map farther south. "Hen duo shan (*Many mountains*)," they said, hands swooping up and down to indicate rise and fall.

"Duo shao xiao shi (*How many hours*)?" I asked – whereupon they asked how long it took me to reach their station. "Si xiao shi (*Four hours*)," I said.

They worked it out between them, and one answered: "Jiu xiao shi." Nine more hours.

Ugh.

Would they let me proceed? I didn't bother finding out. We talked a bit about America and my teaching position; they offered me tart fruit candy; I offered them beans and bananas. Then I wheeled about, faced the rising switchbacks, and began the disappointing trek home.

. . .

COMPOSITION: DESCRIBE THE PERFECT SPOUSE.

FEMALE STUDENT:

If I marry, I hope my spouse is a perfect person like my father. I like my father because he is not only a good father but also a good husband. He is a great man.

My father is a teacher who teaches mathematic. He devotes his life to the education. So I think my spouse will work well. In the future, with the development of the science and technique, the society will need the person who works hard and has technical skill. Of course, he will adapt to the society and have the courage to compete with others. But I don't hope he is a leader in the factory or company.

I hope he will love our family, which is the important part of his life. We love each other deeply. He is a kind hearted man. I hope he can protect me because I am an introvert and sentimental girl. If there is something, I always cry. I hope when I feel happy, he will share pleasure with me; when I feel unhappy, he will let me cry and then console me. I hope there is no quarreling in our lives. If we have something conflicted we can think from the other side.

If we had children, he would love his children and was a good father. He won't be strict with the children's study. But he will lead them to how to study. In his spare time, he may bring the children to go out and have a picnic or parties. When the children do something wrong, he doesn't criticize them but tell them how to realize their mistakes. We have a happy family.

Of course, this is only my hope. In the world, there isn't a perfect person. Perhaps to know each other is a predestined lot. Some day, when I meet a young man, I feel he is a good man, we will marry and live for ever. "Love means you don't have to say you are sorry ever." I believe it.

MALE STUDENT:

She will be lively and lovely. I like lively girl because I'm more quiet than lively. If I marry a girl who is more quiet then I'm afraid our daily life would be too peaceful. And she had better be beautiful. Every man likes beautiful women.

. . .

COME ON, MISTAH HOBISON! You can sing it!" They dragged me to the stage and pressed scribbled lyrics into my hand. With a disco ball splaying colors above me, I began:

> *Xie xie ni gei wo de ai*
> *Jin sheng jin shi wo bu wang huai*
> *Xie xie ni gei wo de wen rou*
> *Ban wo du guo nei ge nian dai*

The refrain was tricky, the verses even tougher, yet they asked me to sing it so many times that I remember the refrain to this day.

To celebrate the end of the semester, students in the professionals section had pooled their money to rent the karaoke room, a facility with flashy lights and plush lounge chairs used primarily for staff parties. I'd tried to reserve a similar room in the winter, only to be pocket vetoed. Obviously my students' collective guanxi exceeded my own.

The night kicked off with American songs – "Star-Spangled Banner," "Billie Jean" and others – and then launched into one Chinese ballad after another. In solos, duets and small ensembles, they eked enjoyment out of every minute of our allotted time. When Wu Li Yan's duet partner left him on the stage early he didn't miss a beat, just picked up her lines in a screechy female voice. No one was permitted to escape karaoke altogether, authority figures least of all. Unfortunately my guitar solo didn't satiate them – I had to flounder through a Mandarin song as well.

The one chosen for my humiliation, "Xiao Fang," chronicled a story from the Cultural Revolution, that political purge when Communists closed schools and sent waves of students to farm the countryside. According to my students, the singer reminisced about a young woman he'd met in his sudden peasantry, only to be transferred away from her and eventually returned to his

Karaoke

spouse. The song thanked the village girl for the temporary companionship that had sustained him.

That this song had been allowed to top the charts in 1994 surprised me, hinting as it did at Communist-inflicted turmoil. Certainly it resonated with my students, who found humor in Lao Wai naively parroting that angst-ridden period when politics had maddened their world.

Near the end of our fourth hour of karaoke a clerk arrived to shut us down. We all took the stage to ring out one last "Country Roads," and then an encore: "Auld Lang Syne" (also known throughout China), sung so mournfully I couldn't resist hyping it with an upbeat tempo and silly jig. We left with exhausted giggles to pack for our departures.

The next day we held a brief certificate ceremony and exchanged contact information. My students included notes with their addresses – final words from my beloved guides and friends.

> *Probably, this special training you gave me is my once-in-lifetime opportunity.*
>
> *I hope you won't forget me and the gift I presented you in your birthday reminds you of remembering me.*
>
> *I wish your life better than mine. Welcome to China again.*
>
> *Thanks a million!*
>
> *Your each feature will be deeply rooted in my mind. Don't forget me!*
>
> *I hope you can get what you want.*

Farewell with grad students

I hope I'll meet you in Beijing during your honeymoon! (This continued a long-running invitation for me to honeymoon with my future wife in Beijing.)

Maybe in future I will go to America. I'll visit you.

You will be in my mind all of my life.

. . .

POWDERY PINK, Chinese inner tubes used a valve unfamiliar in America, neither Schrader nor Presta. At a supply store I bought a slew of extra tubes and brake pads, a patch kit, and a backup pump. Then I noticed a bin of little metal widgets, sort of a cross between a carabiner and a bottle opener.

"Zhe shi shen me?" I asked the shopkeeper, holding one. He charaded its purpose: spoke tightener – ingeniously convenient, capable of being used with just three fingers. I added one to my purchase. Then, as I mounted my bicycle, an idea occurred to me and I hurried back to buy another.

On the way home I stopped by Yang Jin Yu's repair corner. Eying my dilapidated bicycle with his "You again?" smile, he coaxed his knees up from his bench. I offered the spoke tightener with both hands extended: a gift.

I was pleased to see it was new to him – upon my demonstration he gave a clap of delight. How many times had he refused payment for fixing my bicycle, and now to be pleased by such a small gesture!

As I looked back through my photos for this book, I realized that in stature and facial features, Yang bore a resemblance to my own grandfather, who had passed away two years earlier. This similarity, combined with his enthusiastic paternal concern, must have drawn me subconsciously. If only I'd been more fluent in Mandarin – I wished I could have known him better.

. . .

MY LACK OF AN ENDGAME STRATEGY had caught up to me. Patty was wise to duck the responsibility. What to do with my rabbits? They wouldn't make it in the wild, and the prospect of their complementing a stir fry was unacceptable.

Lack of options forced me to weigh an offer from one student. Wanda had always adored my rabbits during Free Talks. Better yet, she tongue-lashed anyone who lifted them by the ears or referred to them as ingredients. A twenty-year-old daughter of Lin Da staff members, Wanda lived on campus, so my rabbits wouldn't need to travel far. When I asked for a promise that they wouldn't be stewed, she seemed even more determined than I was to protect them.

Before heading west I packed my white puffballs in a box, bungeed it to my bicycle rack, and pedaled to Wanda's apartment. Her parents were at work but she introduced me to her grandmother, an ancient woman, stooped and sedentary in the bedroom she shared with her granddaughter.

I unfolded the box flaps to discover my rabbits in trembling fits. The dark swaying had terrified them, perhaps even nauseated them. I felt awful for not considering that; it would have been easy to walk them over.

Whispering reassuringly, Wanda's grandmother bent down, picked up the rabbits one at a time, and cuddled them in her arms until they calmed.

"You see," Wanda said, "she is here by herself and gets lonely. She will take good care of them."

I couldn't have imagined a better arrangement.

. . .

I'D TRAVELED TO CHINA to find a wife. They were certain of it. Every eligible American male sought to barter wealth and a visa for happily-ever-after, so students bragged about women in their work units who would suit me. A few of my female students were perhaps *too* giggly, arriving for Free Talks in their safety groups of five or six.

I sought many things out of that year, but a wife was not among them. Communicating across the cultural divide was tricky enough without mixing in matrimonial concerns.

These thoughts flashed through my mind the moment I recognized the voice on the phone. It was Janet, which was odd – students rarely called. By that point Lin Da was deserted. Why had Janet stuck around?

Apparently to insist: "I need to talk to you."

"Umm, okay …"

"Can I come up?"

Up? "Where are you?"

"In the hotel lobby." So she'd already crossed campus and was calling from the hotel across the court. She sounded tense.

"Why don't I come down there?"

"I need to give you something. We may never see each other. I think I must come up."

"No, that's okay." Best to avoid a one-on-one farewell, the two of us alone in my apartment. "I'll come down. Wait there, okay?" I hung up before she could protest.

Janet had availed herself of most Free Talks and was a regular at office hours. Early twenties. Advanced English. Definitely attractive. Ethical and cross-cultural qualms aside, a bachelor can't receive the flirtations of a pleasing young woman without being at least a little curious. Apparently I hadn't kept that curiosity well enough in check, solidifying her intentions toward me. Alas! – the semester had ended with our anticipated intercontinental romance unkindled.

Before heading downstairs I knocked on fellow teacher Melissa's door. "I'm going down to the hotel lobby to talk to a student I really don't want to talk to," I said. "If I'm not back in twenty minutes, bail me out, will you? Stop by, act like you have to make a long distance call, then come over and talk to us. And *don't leave* until she leaves."

Was Melissa ever curious! "What's going on?"

"Long story. Or actually no story – much ado about nothing. I'll fill you in later."

Janet looked nice in the small couch of the lobby's far corner. She wore her form-fitting purple dress, one of her more flattering outfits. Something in her anxious expression glowed, making me wish for a moment that things didn't have to be as they were. She seemed ready to blossom, and part of me yearned to play that role in her life. It was alluring.

Alluring, and impossible – against the rules of my organization. Besides, in a few weeks I'd be on the other side of the planet. Some people make long-distance relationships work, but *looooong*-distance? Not for me. I ignored the open cushion next to her and sat on the perpendicular couch.

"I want to give this to you," she said, extending a card and small bag. The card gushed in the customarily sappy way about the beautiful semester we'd had together and how she would always hold her memories of me close to her heart, and wished me all the best, and hoped one day our paths would cross again. Students did tend to wax rosy on farewells.

The gift bag contained a framed Glamour Shots-style photo – professional makeup, glowing background, soft focus. Yes, she looked exquisite.

"Well, thank you," I said, unsure what tone to take.

Then it got weird. From her purse she pulled out a picture of herself with another man, and identified him as her fiancé. I hadn't known she was engaged; she'd never mentioned him. "We're going to marry in the winter," she explained.

Good, good, this was good! "Congratulations," I gushed, "that's terrific. He looks like a great guy. I'm sure you'll be very happy together!"

Her downcast face told me that wasn't the right thing to say. She seemed wistful. Was I supposed to be jealous? Tell her to leave him? Proclaim my love? I was blowing whatever lines she'd scripted for this scene.

"So my train leaves tomorrow morning," I said abruptly. "I need to finish packing."

"How will you get your bicycle to the station?"

"I'll ride it. Everything I'm taking fits on the bike. Then I'll take the bike apart and pack it at the station."

"No no no," she said, "that's very complicated. You must take a taxi."

"Too expensive."

"No, you must take a taxi. I'll get one for you."

She matched every strong refusal with even stronger insistence. Thus I failed, and we parted with a plan to meet early the next morning. So much for our farewell.

I made it back upstairs before Melissa's rescue mission. "How'd it go?" she teased.

"I have no idea." I explained what I could, then added, "She told me she's engaged."

"Yeah? Then why's she so fixated on you?"

"Exactly."

At 7AM Janet waited with the taxi, excited, in the same outfit (not unusual in China) but with even more attention to her makeup. I tossed my saddle bags and gear in the back seat, then with the help of the driver loaded my Diamondback in its bag into the trunk.

"Thank you for arranging the taxi," I told Janet. "Enjoy your summer!"

"No, I'm going to the station," she said, and hopped in.

So we rode together to the station, making small talk with awkward silences. She insisted on paying the taxi fare. Then she insisted on translating as I bought my ticket. Then she bought a platform ticket for herself so she could see me off. At each stage I thanked her for the help, but the emotional stakes kept rising. How had I brought this on?

When a conductor opened up the coach I half-dreaded Janet would climb aboard to help me find my seat, but no. I staggered down the tight aisle with my gear and monstrous sack, sighing with relief. No major scene had taken place. We'd said goodbye on the platform, and that was all. Maybe I'd read into things – maybe she really had been only helping. That over, I could begin preparing mentally for the adventure ahead.

I'd splurged on a soft sleeper ticket for the extra storage space. One of my three cabinmates helped me contort my bike's components as I shoved at the bag, trying to squeeze it under a bunk. It wasn't happening. I started to sweat. For weeks I'd dreaded the Diamondback not fitting, prompting a conductor to demand an extra fee to store it in a baggage car. Even if my bike did escape theft, I wouldn't know how to retrieve it at the next station.

Pulse racing – any minute the conductor would check our tickets – I kicked the bag, chain and spokes and gears wrenching against one another until with a groan they slipped under the bunk. I might have broken something, but it could be fixed in Taiyuan. One step at a time.

Reclining in my bunk, I was just about to attempt a conversation with my cabinmates when one of them pointed out the window. Our train hadn't set off yet, and there on the platform stood Janet, waving at me wildly.

Had I forgotten something? Was I on the wrong train? I jolted to the slider and clacked the window open.

"Hello," she said, pleased.

"Hi," I groaned. She was waiting to see the train off.

There we remained, she on the platform, I a few feet up in a coach window with little to say, just grinning awkwardly until whenever it was the train would roll. We crawled through ten such minutes, during which I became increasingly conscious of the impression my cabinmates were developing about this relationship. Occasionally Janet spoke to them in Mandarin and they answered back, leaving me to ask dumbly, "What'd you tell them?"

"I asked them to take good care of you." From their amused smiles it was clear that wasn't all she'd said.

Finally – *finally!* – the wheels cranked into motion.

"Well, this is it," I said. "Thank you for all your help. Take care. Goodbye!"

But even that wasn't it: Janet walked alongside, hurrying with the train. "Goodbye!" she called, "I'll miss you!" Then she was running, running beside my window as the wheels accelerated and she struggled to keep up and finally she fell behind and stopped there, face contorted, waving.

I kept my head out the window for as many seconds as I calculated would be polite, then pulled inside with a half-shudder, half-chuckle. What a scene! I wondered what had brought it on.

My three cabinmates eyed me as though they knew exactly what had brought it on. They grinned at the sly young waiguoren who'd won himself a Chinese girlfriend. There would be no convincing them otherwise – Janet had made sure of that.

To this day I'm not sure what inspired such a Hollywood farewell. Yet another set of signals garbled across the cultural divide, I suppose.

Gansu Grasslands :: Tibetan Buddhist Temple in Langmusi

JOURNEY TO THE WEST

The door was locked. Locked, and this taught me something about my-self: even after buying a mountain bike and tent, after training for weeks, after hauling my gear to Taiyuan to meet up with Chad and Chris – detail-ing our route, inventorying items, shopping for remaining needs, then test-packing our bikes for both road and train, rehearsing breakdown and rebuild until we felt confident we could manage in a crowd – after buying tickets and killing the extra hours downtown until it was time to retrieve our gear and make our way to the rail station and beyond –

– even after all of that, part of me didn't believe the trip would really hap-pen. Nothing *that* unusual happened in my life. Even with its challenges, a year in Beijing had turned out more routine than I would have believed.

So when we discovered that Chris' spare key did not, after all, work in Nicole's door – Nicole, our fellow teacher who'd already departed for Xian on her own adventure, and who had let me use her apartment in her absence – I faced the locked door as destiny. No trip for me.

We scoured the building, looking for the superintendent. The clock ticked down; our train would leave soon. Chad and Chris were ready, bikes packed and poised in the hallway. All my preparations lay behind the door.

"You guys go on," I said. "I can buy another ticket tomorrow. We'll meet up in Xian." Little hope of that: how would I convince the superintendent to let me enter Nicole's apartment? I might as well slink back to Beijing and catch a flight home.

But no, Chad and Chris wouldn't leave me behind – they'd wait it out with me.

"You're being silly," I argued. "There's no reason to throw away *all* our tickets. Go on, I'll find you at Eric's." We'd planned to stay with a fellow teacher stationed in Xian.

They wouldn't budge. We brainstormed: who else on a deserted campus might have a key? Chad half-kicked at the door, a frustrated gesture that gave me an idea. The door had only a locked handle, no deadbolt. Maybe I could jimmy it? The lock didn't seem all that robust.

I slipped a fifty-yuan phone card between door and frame.

The catch popped immediately.

So did Chris' eyes. "Good to know our apartments were secure all year."

"Good to know this phone card was worth something after all," I said. "I never did get it to work."

We sped down the main thoroughfare on laden bikes. The sight of three panicked waiguoren (two of them sandy blonde) dismantling expensive bikes in the middle of the rail station drew a pack of attention so intense a police officer had to use his whistle to carve our way to the platform. Fortunately a delay had kept our train.

Three bikes and gear shouldn't have fit beneath two low bunks, but somehow it worked. We were on our way to Xian, Gateway of the Silk Road.

Chad and I dueled on a magnetic Xianqi set; Chris spoke with a young woman who'd learned English in high school. Smokestacks passed by, then fields, the rich aroma of burnt crop stubble entering the windows. People bicycling or walking near the tracks paused to watch our train. I wondered about their lives, the dozens of histories rushing past.

A glimpse of one woman caught my attention. Atop a grassy knoll with two companions, she bore an uncanny resemblance to Heather, the vinegar connoisseur from Taiyuan. I marvelled at this phenomenon: after an entire year of seeing no two people in China who looked alike, a glance from a moving train revealed similarities, yet also subtle differences in hairstyle and jawline. Perhaps it was no coincidence we were just outside Taiyuan – their features may have been regional.

The landscape wore on into night. I dug out my journal and had just begun jotting down these thoughts when the coach lights switched off.

. . .

OUR TRAIN SQUEALED INTO XIAN at 5:40AM. Bleary, we hauled our bags through the station and out to the dim air, where taxi drivers competed for new arrivals. Amid the bustling pavement we reassembled our bikes. There at my elbow an attractive young woman was offering help.

"Xie xie (*Thank you*)," I said. She was stabilizing the frame so I could lock the wheel nuts.

"You are welcome to Xian," she said. "You'll stay at Flats of Renmin Hotel. We have the best food. Come, I'll get you a taxi."

"Oh, I'm sorry," I answered, "we don't need a taxi. Or a hotel – we're staying with our friend at the Sheraton."

"A taxi will take you to Flats of Renmin Hotel. You won't have to look for it. The food is magnificent, all the foreigners say this. The hotel is very cheap. All the foreigners stay there."

Her beaming smile and charming persistence weren't easy to resist. Still, I asked, "Why should we stay there if we have somewhere to stay for free?"

"You'll love it. You'll delight in Dad's Home Cooking." She presented me a business card that introduced her as Eliza of Dad's Home Cooking: Featuring Western Cuisine.

Bikes complete, Chad and Chris braced to go. I slid onto my seat and pushed a little forward with one foot. "Across the street from the hotel," Eliza added hastily. "I will see you there." I glanced back to see her homing in on some other waiguoren.

We headed to the historic district inside Xian's ancient wall, then met up with Eric, who had a remarkably sweet gig at the Sheraton. Responsible for the English skills of all staff members, Eric enjoyed free reign of the hotel. He walked us through the kitchen to flaunt his Western diet ("I can order anything from the menu, three meals a day"), past the gym where he exercised, then past the snack shop.

"You don't have to leave the hotel for anything!" we exclaimed.

"It's been a bit tough," he admitted, "connecting with the culture. Some-

Street cutting through Xian's historic wall

167

times you just get comfortable." He brought us up the elevator to his room. We took turns in a real shower, with the water both hot and under pressure. "Unfortunately I can't have you stay here," he apologized. "It's against my contract, and I want to respect that – they've been good to me. But I know a great place that everyone loves: The Flats of Renmin."

"That's funny." I fished Eliza's business card from my pocket. "We just met someone from there."

"Yeah, the restaurant across the street has a girl who works the morning trains. It's no Sheraton, but everyone who stays there likes it."

At the city center we met up with Nicole of the locked door and her teammate Christine K. for a lunch of streetside baozi. Then we retrieved our gear from Eric's room and checked in at The Flats of Renmin, an older facility teeming with backpackers from America, Europe and Australia.

As promised, facing the hotel we found Dad's Home Cooking, a bare-bones yet innovative joint that cooked up decent approximations of Western specialties like burgers, omelets and muesli, which I slurped for the dairy. A scruffy, middle-aged man with a hint of girth, Dad capitalized on the backpacker influx by catering to their roughing-it culture. Worn wooden tables offered outdoor dining; a chalkboard menu and wire-suspended bulbs rounded out the feel. Dad reveled in the personalities that patronized him, nomadic spirits that kept him young.

When we first rolled in, Eliza sat at our table and demanded our story. She was Dad's daughter. They worried about competition affecting them, for Dad the Entrepreneur was haunted. Two spots down another restaurant had opened: Mum's Home Cooking. A blatant replica, Mum's had a bit more startup capital (red plastic tablecloths, tinted lighting) and an edge in cleanli-

Eliza and Dad (standing in the foreground)

ness. From his own shaded spot, Dad eyed his doppelgangers with heartache and plugged on.

After dinner I pedaled through Xian's evening heat, stopping to watch billiard players at a grid of tables beneath a mammoth tent. When I returned to the hotel, Eliza spotted me coasting down the dark street. "Our restaurant needs a new sign," she said.

"Yes?"

"Will you help us make it?"

I scrunched my face. "A lit sign? I wouldn't have the first idea –"

"No, we have wood and paint, we just need help with the English."

"Oh." Smart people, tapping into available resources. "What have you got so far? What do you want to say? Here, let me see a menu." Eliza beckoned Dad to the counter and translated his thoughts.

Less than eighteen hours in Xian, I was helping to hammer out a marketing message for a local restaurant.

. . .

TAI GUI LE – eighty yuan for a taxi to the Terracotta Warriors?

The bus wasn't that much cheaper, so I filled my water bottles, stuffed my backpack with map, bananas and peanuts, and pedaled out. Three hours each way made for a long day. The next was just as busy, poking through Xian's historic district and shopping for souvenirs with fellow teachers.

Sapped from the late night heat, I stopped by Dad's for a midnight bowl of muesli. Eliza joined me. Did she and her father never stop working?

"We were watching for you all this time," she said. "Will you help us paint the new sign?" They distrusted their ability to print English naturally.

Owl on bike :: Cycling to the Terracotta Warriors

I could sympathize: my Chinese handwriting looked deranged.

"Sure, but I've got to sleep. How about tomorrow?"

"Tomorrow is Saturday. You said you'll leave Saturday."

"Yes, but I promise I'll help before I go."

I intended to fulfill this promise first thing in the morning, but Chad and Chris pointed out that we needed to buy our train tickets early. Afterward we lost time searching for a post office to mail souvenirs home. We still hadn't succeeded when our departure neared.

"Forget it," Chad said, tense. We'd almost missed one train already. "We can mail them from the next town."

We beat it to the hotel to grab our gear. Across the street I noticed Eliza bussing a table and remembered: the sign.

I could do it. No train actually left on time, did it? "Go ahead," I told my partners, "I'll be right behind you."

"What are you *doing*?"

"I promised I'd help Dad with something."

They frowned; I was crazy. And now, already late as I bent over an A-frame sign forming one careful letter after another, Dad and Eliza counting on my work to help with their livelihood, I had to concentrate on each stroke to counteract my trembling hands.

Near the bottom I panicked and only traced the final words. "You'll have to finish, just make it darker, I've got to go." After quick hugs from Eliza and Dad, I bolted to the station, collapsed my bike in record time and reached my hard sleeper bunk above Chad and Chris just two minutes before the train set out. Too close for comfort, but I couldn't help smiling. I'd kept my promise.

Marketing in a hurry

. . .

一
百
七
十
一

MIANZIBAO!"

Her voice called from somewhere uphill, distant yet clear above the street's din. Later I spotted her: a lone woman wearing a wraparound satchel stuffed with newspapers. She progressed slowly, singing out every fifteen seconds: "Mianzibao!" Despite the creases in her face, her voice issued in crystalline alto, sonorous and clean. I anticipated each of her calls as she passed downhill and beyond earshot.

After debarking the overnight train in the town of Lüeyang, we'd pedaled several blocks already humming in the morning hours with pedestrians and bicyclists when we hit a snag. Chris' saddlebags rattled against her spokes; they needed reinforcing. As we waited for a tailor shop to open we grabbed a breakfast of hardboiled eggs, rice and steamed bread.

We parked in a convenient gap between shops, a razed nook that accommodated our bikes within the shelter of three mossy brick walls. While a worker improved the saddlebags, Chad and Chris searched for a post office, leaving me to guard the gear. Unfortunately this little recess functioned like a stage, framing Lao Wai's presence for passersby. A crowd of mostly men assembled into a human arc from one brick corner to the other, staring at our bikes, our packs, me. Initially one of the tailors shooed them away, but he either lost interest or gave up in futility.

Time passed; the wall of attention didn't. I supposed I was their first waiguoren, but that didn't make the caged gorilla feeling any less uncomfortable. Didn't they need to be anywhere? To distract myself I wrote in my journal.

Tight alley and bamboo scaffolding, Lüeyang

一百七十二

New friends ::
Following the river

Nowhere to camp ::
Hotel guests

Half an hour later Chad and Chris shoved back through to me. We had to walk our bikes out of the gathering to get enough space to mount.

One final check of our bikes and gear, and then we looked at each other. Braced ourselves. Inhaled.

"Zou ba," Chad announced. We were off.

We passed beyond Lüeyang's buildings to simpler housing, then to villages, and finally to open fields. The sky warmed, blue and bright with a hint of humidity. After my many circles around Beijing's mountains, this was what I'd craved: an unwritten script, no good idea of what would come next.

We dodged the midday heat with a xiuxi at a river crossing where women scrubbed clothes against the rocks. Our swimming earned the attention of a handful of locals, including one polite elderly man in a straw hat who requested that I take his photo. Observing my rock-skipping efforts, a younger man about my age coached me into better results through a more decisive wrist snap. Something about the gentle simplicity of these people endeared me to them.

We cycled the rest of that afternoon, and near dusk noted a slight village – more of a forested truck stop, really – named Jinjiahe. The dense trees offered little in the way of a tent site, so we pushed on. The road ascended, tracing a creek through close walls, and degraded from gravel to dirt. The walls pulled in tighter; darkness threatened. "This is crazy," Chad muttered. "There's nowhere to set up camp. Let's go back."

Night had settled by the time we'd rattled back down the slope to Jinjiahe, but that didn't stop a gaggle of children from noticing us. They hovered at our waists as we entered the office of the concrete two-story hotel to arrange a room – four yuan per night, less than half the cost of a jar of peanut butter in Beijing. When the manager led us upstairs, children badgered us into letting them carry our bags and bicycles … and when she unlocked our door, they poured into our room before we did!

Drained at the close of our first full day, we found ourselves playing host to 21 children bouncing on our beds, poking at our gear, and peppering us with questions. I shared from my stash of Da Bai Tu (*Big White Rabbit*) candy, a milky taffy wrapped in edible rice paper, and became smitten by a buttonish six-year-old with twinkling eyes and bowlcut hair. Fascinated yet bashful, she hid behind younger children, "protecting" them with an arm wrapped around their necks.

A gentleman knocked on our door. His home was only a few minutes' walk away; would we care to join his family for a meal? By that point it was almost 10PM, but we couldn't refuse such graciousness. We followed him and were treated to a hot meal of noodles with egg and tomato prepared by his sister, mother and grandmother in the late night.

Stars dripped between overhead branches as we shuffled back to the hotel, beyond exhausted – only to entertain more children (where were their parents?). The hotel manager and a passing truck driver dropped in to talk, left awhile, returned again. Was it our red, half-shut eyes or our nodding heads that finally convinced the manager we needed rest? Laughing, she swatted the children's shoulders and ordered them out. Sleep crashed in fast and deep.

. . .

EITHER IT WAS SUMMER VACATION in Jinjiahe, or morning classes had been suspended so every child could see us off. I handed out more Da Bai Tu candies, giving some extras to the little girl whose shy spirit had stolen my heart.

The prior evening's switchbacks weren't any easier the second time up, especially in the morning's rising heat. After two solid hours of low-gear work we rested, eating crackers and peanut butter at a grassy bend and watching the rare truck or bus.

The opposite slope presented a different challenge: the choppy surface that had annoyed us on ascent took some white knuckle nerve at a downhill clip. When a particularly ugly bump jounced my camera from its pouch, its palm-fitting angles proved conducive to road travel – it tumbled end over end, easily pacing my bike for what must have been two hundred feet. Amazingly, the shutter still clicked, but my heart sank. Could I trust it? No choice, really – we were far from any photography shop. For the remainder of the

Homes outside Jinjiahe :: Switchbacks

trip I drank in each sight as though its retinal impression would be all I had to remember.

Where the road flattened, farmers spread out wheat stalks to be threshed by passing trucks. After each, family members flipped the stalks and waited many minutes for the next truck. Our bike tires played their own small role in the harvest, but no one flipped the stalks after we passed.

Then Chad vomited. He confessed that he'd woken that morning nauseous, and had kept mum about it to avoid worrying us. The heat? Something he ate? I had no idea how he'd managed the morning switchbacks, and wondered again about the wisdom of our enterprise. Anything at all could derail us. We stopped beside a trickling waterfall to splash ourselves cool and take a xiuxi. Chad and Chris sprawled in the grass; I tracked the water uphill and gave my knee a pretty gash in some thorny brush.

Further on a sign announced Gansu, a province that, based on the asphalt's sudden smoothness, commanded a significantly larger budget for roads. Soon we entered a small town, the first since pedaling out of Lüeyang a day and a half earlier. Chad and Chris attracted the most attention, and as the customary gathering encircled us I rolled backwards and away for a rare perspective: *outside* the eyeball ring. I called others to ogle my blonde friends – "Waiguoren, lai zhe, kuai dianr, kan (*come here, quickly, look*)!"

One man noticed my bloody knee, asked me to stay put, and hustled off. Minutes later he returned with a medical bag. He insisted on treating my injury with iodine and a bandage. What kindness!

"Duo yuan xia yi cheng (*How far to the next town*)?" I asked him.

"Mei you cheng (*No town*)," he replied. "Mei you jiu dian, mei you can

Threshing wheat :: Small town

guan (*No hotel, no restaurant*)."

It was 4PM. With plenty of daylight remaining we forged ahead. The road rose in a long, moderate slope that we crested around dusk. We could have pitched tent near the top, but we yearned for another warm meal, so we rolled down the other side, hoping to hit a town at the bottom.

Halfway down the sun abandoned us. Without streetlights, moon or stars, we hurtled downhill through the murky blur between road and sky. At times, without warning, invisible wheat hissed beneath our tires. This isn't safe, I kept wanting to object; one of us is going to spill. Chad, in the lead, flew on, wind rushing across his ears – no way he would hear me, and I wasn't about to accelerate to catch him.

Much, much later than we'd estimated, out of the blanket dimness ahead glimmered the lights of Kang Xian. We stowed our bikes in a hotel for nine yuan per night, then followed a woman who volunteered to escort us to a decent restaurant. A clothing sales representative, she'd been raised in far-north Harbin until the age of eight, and now was raising a thirteen-year-old son in western China. The restaurant manager set us up in a private room and brought out an array of fabulous dishes, every one of them a knockout, including the best gong bao ji ding I'd tasted all year.

Of course, sunbaked and famished as we were, anything would have tasted fabulous.

. . .

THUD THUD THUD: police at the door, interpreter in tow. It wasn't even 8AM.

Groggily we produced our IDs and explained our travel plans. The interpreter handed us a carbon copy form on which we crammed our names, teaching institutions and home addresses. (I wonder if somewhere in China a central file still details my many police check-ins.)

Later, over bean paste buns, Chad spread out our map. "Chris and I have been talking," he said. "We're here" – he pointed at a long valley, then stretched his finger farther across the mountains – "and we should be here. I didn't expect this many switchbacks."

"And I've got my plane to catch," Chris said. She would be flying home early to attend a friend's wedding.

"Can't you just grab a train wherever we're at?" I asked.

"How many stations have you seen?"

Oh. Good point.

"We need to make Lanzhou in two weeks, and we won't do it on bike."

Was our adventure to end so soon? Chad saw my expression. "I'm not saying we won't bike at all," he reassured. "We just need to leapfrog this part, then we'll see what happens."

My resentment over buying bus tickets turned into gratitude when the bus launched into an unabated, hour-upon-hour climb up the next mountain range. Two fellow passengers, instructors at a local university, offered to guide us through the next town. During this conversation Chad glanced out the window at the interminable incline, then back at me as if to say, "You see?" We'd dodged a bullet.

At a rare stretch of level ground the bus stopped, the door opened, and men poured out to urinate on a rock ledge. They'd been drinking tea in glass jars the whole trip; so had the women, but none of them exited for relief. Sacrificing comfort for modesty? I felt sorry for them.

"This is the top," one of our Chinese counterparts explained, "the, neige, the summit. We make this trip many times. The whole way after is down."

Chad, Chris and I looked at each other. "*All* down? How far?"

"Maybe forty kilometers."

The sun was still high: plenty of time. We pulled our bags off the bus and started assembling.

"But this is not necessary!" protested our new acquaintances. "You paid for your tickets. Wudu is a long way. It will be dark before you arrive." Our premature exit had them stammering with disappointment. We weren't on this trip to build guanxi, though, so we shrugged it off. The driver honked. One of the men pressed his business card in my hands: "Call us when you reach Wudu!" A roar of exhaust left us free.

We coasted past mountains of orange dirt and rock carved, base to crest, into staircase-like terraces. Most were barren, but a few watercolor splashes

Assembling bikes :: Terraces

一
百
七
十
八

of green showed current use. Who eked out their sustenance from this land-scape? How many decades had it taken to stagger out the colossal relics through which we sped?

Later the terrain changed to a gray ravine with homes peeking out of caves. Later still we crossed an area of freestanding homes with mud walls and thatched roofs. We coasted on, pedals relaxed, geographical variations scrolling by effortlessly.

Thatched houses began to clump together: a village. A truck approached, and too late Chad noticed a bent woman stepping from a ditch into the road. At our speed there wasn't time to stop – Chad veered to the far side – the woman, startled by his speed and with the truck upon her, jerked backwards – straight into my path.

I don't know how I missed her without spilling. I don't know how Chris, behind me, missed her too. It was all so fast, the village already behind us, another glorious gorge opening ahead, the sky still brilliant. Go back and apologize? I couldn't imagine a way past the waiguoren issue. I concentrated on breathing normally. Still rolling behind me, Chris was crying.

We leaned on our brakes after that.

Near dusk the road leveled out – time to resume pedaling. The sky had dimmed by the time we reached Wudu's hilly streets. No one suggested call-ing the university instructors. Instead we found a ten-yuan hotel room and a restaurant for noodles with beef and tomatoes, plus gong bao rou ding, my staple dish with pork instead of chicken ("Branch out a little, will ya?" Chris chided).

At the hotel I discovered my Achilles tendon swollen and bleeding through

Mao shrine :: Wudu

the sock – a pedal had clipped me when I'd dodged the elderly woman. I soaked my ankle in the sink and thanked God nothing worse had occurred.

. . .

THE BUS WEST wouldn't leave until 2PM, so we coasted up and down Wudu's streets, exploring. The restaurant where we lunched featured a Mao shrine, a bit unusual in a locale so far from Beijing. In the sui bian atmosphere of these small towns we felt the truth of the Chinese proverb "The mountains are high and the emperor is far away." Did locals consider this restaurant's display of Mao veneration odd? Or was the shrine a bit of retro flair, a "back in the day" touch for ambiance?

An approaching ice cream truck played a tinny version of "Here Comes the Bride." Where it stopped, people emerged from doorways carrying plastic bags, which a worker loaded into the back – a garbage truck.

Back at the terminal a clerk directed us to a bus with sacks of watermelons on its roof rack; a woman planned to sell them in the next town. Our driver demanded that we stow our bikes and gear up there as well. We bungee corded our belongings into place as securely as possible, rattling them to make sure they were switchback- and pothole-proof, nestled there among the watermelons.

The road followed a shallow valley with a wide river. At times it narrowed to dangle just above the water, gravel slope angling toward the plunge. Clouds obscured the taller mountain peaks. Much of this area would have been easy pedaling along rice fields, but lunch wasn't settling with my stomach, so I curled in my seat with abdominal cramps and appreciated, for the

Wudu :: Bikes and watermelons

second time in two days, our vehicular cheating.

Our bus sputtered to a stop in the middle of a valley of rice paddies. The driver and handler poked under the hood for the better part of an hour as the rest of us kicked gravel and stared at damp green rectangles.

When the engine finally cranked back to life we finished that stretch of valley – low, grass-padded mountains with dark veins hinting at coal – to arrive under a chilly rain in Zhugqu. *Zhug* looked odd; Mandarin didn't end syllables with the letter G. Was the town's name Tibetan? This region belonged to the mainland but skirted close enough to Tibet that we hoped for signs of a radically different culture.

Already 5PM and with the rain unrelenting, we opted against biking. A young teen with one arm in a sling insisted on helping me with my gear. He waited as we secured a hotel room, then carried my bike up two flights. Between the rain and the brimming river outside our door, we would have plenty of white noise to lull us to sleep.

I was about to surrender in bed to stomach angst when a police officer entered our room. No twenty-something easily snowed with a smile, this officer wore a uniform distended from his aging bulk. His eyes squinted, neck bulged; his forehead beaded with sweat. A whiff publicized his intoxication. Obviously displeased, he recorded the information from our IDs, then exited without a word. Were we in trouble?

Undeterred by the downpour, Chad left to scope out the town; Chris and I played cards as I waited for my discomfort to subside. Two young couples visited for an awkward bout of conversation, followed by a pair of middle school girls who just giggled at the door. By that point night had fallen and my system was ready to expurgate. I descended both flights to the hotel rest-

*Village rising from
the mud*

room – and immediately walked back up.

"That was quick," Chris remarked.

"It's pitch black in there," I said, rummaging though my saddlebags for a flashlight. "I can't even find the hole." Tactile detection was out of the question.

When I returned I found a note: Chad and Chris had left for the dining room on the first floor. I joined them for some plain rice. In the middle of our meal the intoxicated officer entered the room and sat a few tables away. Trapped, we shoveled our food and tried to make ourselves inconspicuous.

Fat chance: the other men at the officer's table pointed us out. To our dismay he stepped over and plopped into the fourth seat at our table. Gone were the gruff demeanor and odor of alcohol. In fact he now smiled jovially. Making up for his earlier appearance? He asked about our travel plans with genuine interest, and informed us almost paternally that rain would muddy the roads through the next day.

That would mean yet another bus. Rats.

As he lingered at our table, squeezing out whatever laughter was possible across our different languages, we came to enjoy his company. He told stories like a favorite uncle. Just before leaving, however, his tone became serious. We were fine to be in his town, but we would need to watch ourselves. Culturally, the next town was Tibetan – and therefore closed to foreigners.

. . .

BUS NUMBER SAN. I resisted the temptation to stare at one passenger near the front, a shaven-headed young man wearing a vibrant crimson robe. I'd never seen a Tibetan Buddhist monk in person, and noted with irony this one's styl-

Hotel on the river, Zhugqu

Chris Orvis

Rock slide

Squatties :: Unloading the bus

Wooden housing with prayer flags above

ish wire glasses and digital wristwatch. Also aboard were two women in black Islamic shawls. We'd ventured far enough from traditional Han Chinese areas that other cultures were appearing.

Our seven-hour slog through rain and mud was interrupted at one point by fallen rock. Every able-bodied person got out to shove the debris further down the slope. I found this adventurous; the others' nonchalance suggested it was par for this road.

With few settlements in this section of valley, our driver stopped us for lunch at a lonely plank shack. Dim, musty and immediately overcrowded, its only customers must have been involuntaries like ourselves. Tea arrived local style: a bowl with a fist-sized sugar crystal that sweetened as it dissolved.

Before returning to the bus I stopped by the restroom. The holes weren't separated by privacy dividers, and the room was crowded – no way could I squat knee to knee with other men. "Just go in there and take care of business," Chad admonished. I had to laugh: after teasing Mom about the restroom at the Forbidden City, I deserved this.

The rain finally subsided about an hour from Diebu. As soon as the bus parked we assembled our bikes and beat it out of town in case a No Waiguoren rule really was enforced. I would have liked to explore; with their flags and vivid reds and blues, the shops were more vibrant than those in Beijing. Police officers monitored several intersections, but no one stopped us. I chuckled at a bicyclist who did a double-take on seeing us and ran straight into a barrel.

On the far side of Diebu we hit a police checkpoint, then another twenty minutes later. Our guts tightened as we approached each, but the officers waved us on after inspecting our IDs. All that suspense and intrigue over nothing.

Infrequent farms nestled among these stubby mountains of ragged trees and grass. Where we paused to adjust our gear, a donkey watched from a wooden corral. I stroked its nose and fed it a Da Bai Tu candy. A passing rain cloud forced us to shelter beneath a tree, then treated us to a rainbow.

Thin banners of white and red began to dot the hills in parallel rows of a hundred or more. "They're printed with prayers," Chad explained. "The wind puts them in motion, sending the prayers to … well, not heaven. Buddha, or the gods, I guess."

At a bridge crossing a group of school-age monks were undressing for a swim. They danced around our bikes, pleading that we photograph them. The thought of their faces being seen on the other side of the planet must have tickled them.

Chris Orvis

*Young monks ready to swim ::
Picnic*

Chris Orvis

*Prayer wheel (the high socks
were for sun protection) ::
Unlit goods shop*

Gradually the mountains wore down to stubs. As the sunlight faded we walked our bikes to the far side of a hillock, where we pitched tent out of view of the road and feasted on spam, fruit, dry noodles and peanut butter. The temperature plummeted, taking care of the mosquitoes.

I crawled into my sleeping bag, utterly fatigued, but my friends' voices urged me back out of the tent: "You've got to see this." With zero light pollution and a moonless sky, the Milky Way spilled from one set of hilltops to the other. We lay in our bags on the cool grass and counted satellites crossing the stars.

. . .

AFTER LOADING CAMP back onto our bikes, we cycled through pine-thick mountains interspersed with prayer flags, animal corrals and wooden plank homes. Two women lounged in a grassy meadow, their rich complexions and braided hair reminding me of historic photographs of Native Americans.

At one housing compound, a sizable ornate box perched above a trickling creek. "It's a prayer wheel," Chad explained, pointing at the rotor in the current beneath. "Inside the box is a scroll of prayers – the water sends them on their way."

We bought fruit from a farmer's wagon beside the road, the only commerce opportunity of the morning, and later washed it in a column of falling water in a rocky crevice. Then, since our last shower had been back in Xian, we took turns ducking into the nook with a bar of camp soap to scrub.

By midday we came upon a restaurant attached to an unlit goods shop. Children and men shuffled their feet in the dusty parking area; when we chose a table they filed in and sat at tables to watch. Not to order – just watch. We wolfed our food, then bought snacks from the shop as children pointed out their favorite candies.

That turned out to be civilization's last gasp. Aside from the road, the next region looked untouched, devoid even of the infrequent truck. Yet as we ground out twist after twist beside the river I expected an industrial plant ahead. The sky had turned grim: despite an otherwise resplendent day, a dark patch hovered directly overhead. The road's silence didn't make sense – the high-altitude smog suggested a sizeable factory that would generate *some* traffic, not the utter stillness of this valley. Still, the sky was smeared. China's leniency toward environmental abuse, especially of an otherwise pristine area like this one, angered me.

I sped up to Chad and Chris to vent. "Can you believe the pollution?"
They blinked. "Pollution?"

"There," I pointed up. "You haven't noticed?"

They regarded me as though I'd lost my mind. "That's not pollution," Chris said. "It's … well … space."

No.

The blurry disc above us was so impossibly dark blue it approached black. I braked to stare. No stars shone through as indisputable proof, yet I could think of no other explanation for what my eyes were seeing. At the sky's absolute zenith, blue faded toward black. Could a combination of high elevation and pure air make this possible? Looking straight off the planet toward the cosmos dizzied me.

That was the only day I noticed this phenomenon. I threw back my head often, soaking it in.

The road continued tracking the river's curls, a circuitous exercise that began to feel like a maze. Mountain shoulders cut every view ahead. After some hours the pines fell away and the valley widened, allowing a bit more of a view – but with the air stagnant, gravel coals beneath us and the sun hammering down from its empty sky, we became restless for an exit. No shade existed here. As the mountains whittled down in height we expected to break through, yet the road meandered blisteringly on.

Then we rounded one mountain to face a daunting wall of red rock, ridiculously vertical. A hundred feet of stone above, tiny trees sprouted along the ridge, just across from a coasting bird of prey.

We paused, dismayed by the mountains' second wind.

At least the cliff provided shade. We lay in its cool cover for an overdue xiuxi. An hour later we stretched, mounted, rounded the wall's far edge – a breeze picked up – and were stunned by open grasslands! The cliff had been a topographical border, a sort of natural fence between one landscape and the

Land without shade

next.

Chad's next words cut short our relief: "This looks like where I met the dogs."

My mind shifted to high alert. As we pedaled I scanned the surrounding slopes obsessively. I'd dreaded this area all the way back in Beijing. Imagine, then, how my heart lurched when, without warning, my Diamondback skidded to a violent stop, nearly throwing me.

One of my saddlebag brackets had given out, yanking the corner into my rear wheel. It snapped two spokes and bent a third, leaving an airy gap that looked bad. I hadn't thought to carry extra spokes.

"You think it's rideable?" I asked, gulping down a vision of walking my bike through canine-infested grasslands.

"Can't hurt it much worse to try," Chad said. Thankfully the rear wheel wobbled only slightly; I was still mobile.

As the day ended we crossed a bristly slope to set up camp. Mosquitoes rained on us, making assembly difficult as we slapped every second. What did they normally feed on, here in this field without large animals?

A gentle rain misted the land that night. No dogs materialized out of my hyperactive imagination, but we were awoken several times by the grunting of some groundhoggish critter burrowing near our tent.

. . .

AN INDUSTRIAL TRUCK STOPPED to watch us push our bikes back through the bristles to the road. The men in the cab beckoned, offering us a ride. "Xiahe?" Chad asked, naming the next major town. They nodded.

Hitchhiking! We lifted our bikes into the canvas-covered bed and were bracing ourselves to set out when the men invited Chris to join them in the

Rock wall :: Open grasslands

187

一百八十八

Hitchhiking ::
Tibetan Buddhist temple from
mosque tower

Chris Orvis

Chris Orvis

Prayer wheels :: Mosque

Chris Orvis

cab. They chatted cheerfully up there as Chad and I rattled with the gear.

At a roadblock our driver slowed to wave at the police officers. Before we picked up speed again, two men, one a crimson-robed monk, hopped in back with us. I don't know whose eyes were more surprised, ours or theirs, upon discovering each other.

Sooner than expected we rolled into town. I frowned at the map; it wasn't even noon. "I think we took a wrong turn after the roadblock," I said. "This can't be Xiahe."

Our driver confirmed it: we were in Langmusi, several kilometers south of the road we needed to follow. A communication error? We didn't bemoan our luck for long – a towering mosque beside an equally towering Tibetan Buddhist temple begged to be explored.

We made our way toward them on streets of grass and gravel virtually void of vehicles. The pedestrians, based on their clothing, included Tibetans, Muslims, Han Chinese, perhaps even other groups. This quiet town of unkempt spaces and different cultures fascinated us.

Roughly pyramidal in shape, the Tibetan Buddhist temple flew lines of colored flags from spire to corners. A long row of prayer wheels enabled supplicants to cast prayers by the dozens via flicks of the wrist. In contrast the mosque appeared almost Gothic in its steep, gargoylesque rooflines – yet its prayer hall glowed with sunlight illuminating an ornate rug. We were invited in as long as we removed our shoes.

We exited to monks and children clustered around our bikes. One monk clenched his hood around his face, peering at us through a narrow slit. Did he suffer from a disfigurement? I wondered if he hid his face at all times, or only in the presence of strangers (especially waiguoren – I well understood the raised stakes). How difficult to bear a facial disfigurement in a culture based on face!

A chilly rain blew in, so we opted to stay the night. The windows of the hotel we found used shutters instead of glass. We took a stab at firing up the coal heater, only to abandon the effort when it filled our room with a noxious smell. We must have been doing it wrong, but still – thinking back to the coal-heated hutongs I'd seen in Beijing, I wondered at the tradeoff residents accepted for winter heat.

Evening ushered in the reality of our off-route stranding. Our room offered little relief from the cold. The pit beneath the hotel restroom brimmed visibly. A restaurant served us soppy egg noodles with a few human hairs. Nevertheless, several children cheered our hearts by joining our table and teaching us to count in Tibetan.

Walking from Langmusi ::
On the move

Chris Orvis

Waiguoren ordered off ::
Shops

. . .

MAKING UP FOR LOST TIME, we woke at 6AM to cycle through the brisk air back to where the truck had diverted us. We passed a group of Tibetans – different generations, including a preteen boy and a weathered grandfather – wearing what must have been their Sunday best. Farther down the road walked another family in similar dress. Off to worship, we supposed, but where? These grasslands looked empty. Only the intersection seemed reachable on foot, and that by a long haul.

Already dusty again after the night's rain, the vacant intersection was marked by no signage, just four monks who squatted, waiting. We waited too. I dug out my Frisbee and threw with the monks, all young adults who were more dexterous than their robes suggested.

Before long an industrial truck arrived and invited us aboard, monks and waiguoren alike. A family of three already sat in the bed. Where were they all going?

This truck lacked a canopy. Speeding past velvet slopes beneath the crisp sky, air cooled from the rains, was glorious. But soon the truck stopped at a set of shops, and the driver ordered us off. A checkpoint lay ahead, and he didn't want to be found carrying waiguoren.

This rinky-dink gathering of vendors in the middle of the grasslands bustled with monks, Tibetans, and Han Chinese. Every few minutes another truck of hitchhikers rolled in or set out, all headed north. With nowhere to go but forward, we followed them on bike, brainstorming ways to deal with the checkpoint. Perhaps we could roll around it, behind the slopes?

As we pedaled, trucks filled with well-clad or crimson-robed Tibetans continued to pass by. We gestured to the drivers but they ignored us; one slowed only to say he wouldn't pick up waiguoren. Finally a truck overflowing with people stopped. The handler in the back asked if we wanted to ride.

Preposterous – there wasn't room. Yet the handler assured us they could make space, and the faces in the back seemed not entirely unwilling. We agreed and began lifting our bikes.

"Si shi kuai (*Forty bucks*)," the handler said, indicating our bikes and gear. Extremely pricey! But a truck was our best means past the checkpoint ahead, so I forked over the money and raised my bike to those already aboard, who hauled it in. Chad and Chris were readying their bikes and I was just about to climb up myself when the driver called out from the cab: "Si shi kuai yi ge ren (*Forty bucks per person*)."

One hundred twenty yuan! Had the driver jacked the price because we'd

Truck in the grasslands ::
With Chad, handler, carcass

Chris Orvis

Full truck ::
Young hitchhiker

Chris Orvis

failed to haggle? The most actual bus seats had cost us was ¥28 each for a seven-hour trip.

No other trucks were stopping. Either this crew knew someone at the checkpoint, or they were so itchy for money they were willing to risk it. Of course they could always jettison us, sans refund, if the police raised an eyebrow. But something important was transpiring – an entire tide of people was flowing north. Two more trucks passed as we hesitated. Whatever was going on, we wanted to be swept up in it. So Chad and Chris forked over their money, and bodies squeezed in tighter to make room.

Twenty-three people sat on their bags in the truck bed, including the handler and us. Three monks, six children. Men in brown tunics hemmed in colored bands; women in vibrant prints that didn't exactly match. And suspended from a sidewall, the skinned carcass of a … pig? Dog? What *was* that, anyway?

An elderly couple took turns spinning a handheld prayer wheel attached to a weighted chain. Some people slept; few chatted. From their worn expressions I gathered most had been aboard longer than just that morning. Although they regarded us with curiosity, something larger than three waiguoren occupied their minds.

The checkpoint turned out to be another nonissue. An officer raised his face above the side, glanced at us, and waved the driver on.

About midday our truck paused in a town with dirt streets and a few free-roaming pigs. One fellow passenger lit a cigarette, took a drag, then handed it to his preschool son, who took a drag and handed it back. The boy's thin fingers handled the cigarette deftly; his father took on a mild expression of pride over this manly bonding. I may have guessed the boy's age wrong – perhaps his growth was stunted already.

Some passengers hopped down and crossed the street to a small shop. "You want anything?" I asked my partners, then went in to buy crackers and drinks. I pocketed the change, exited the shop, and the truck was gone.

Not up the street; not down the street. Gone.

I hadn't been inside long – where were the people I'd followed? Where had the truck parked? I walked ahead two blocks: nothing. Fast jog around the block, checking side streets: nothing.

My waist pack was on that truck – to relieve my chafed belly I'd taken to stuffing it in a saddlebag. My bike, possessions … all my money save for the few bills in my pocket … my ID, passport, friends …

Fifteen minutes passed. Why hadn't Chad and Chris stopped the driver? Surely even now they were tongue-lashing him into turning around. If nothing else they'd convince him to pull over so they could come back for me on bike. I didn't know how they would manage a third gear-strapped bike, but they'd figure it out. I sat on the curb in front of the shop and prayed.

Ten more minutes passed. Twenty.

Suppose the truck doesn't return, my thoughts raced. You've got no money, no ID. You don't even know what town this is.

Find a police officer. Ask for an interpreter, a local English teacher to help you contact the embassy in Beijing. Have them contact Mom to wire money ... but how will you receive it without understanding the banking system? Find a waiban ... doubtful in a town so remote, so find a bus to a city with a waiban, perhaps Lanzhou ... but how will you pay for a bus? Beg for help, for someone to do whatever it'll take to move you one leg at a time until you're home.

I stifled the urge to cry. Fantasy, all of it. The truck would return.

I checked the store clock: nearly an hour. I ate the crackers I'd bought for Chad and Chris.

This really is happening to me. My heart weakened; tears boiled out. I really am stranded here with no money and no ID in a place I can't even name. What in the world was I thinking, going on this trip? I asked the clerk for the name of the town. Gainan. At least I had that.

I dared myself to start walking. Give up on the truck. Find a police officer. Sitting here will drive you crazy. You need to move, take charge, act. Just a few more minutes and I would do it. Leave the store. A few more minutes.

The truck pulled up as if nothing had happened. "Sorry about that," Chad called. "They needed to get repairs."

More trucks ::
Gainan

"And just *left* me?" I couldn't mask my emotions – I felt silly, relieved, embarrassed and angry all at once.

Outside the shop, a couple rose from a table and boarded our truck. So did a woman across the street who'd been reading a newspaper. They were the passengers I'd followed, and they'd been around me the entire time – I just hadn't recognized them. During the drive I'd been watching the landscape outside the truck, not the faces within.

"They said we could eat lunch here," Chad explained. "You didn't hear them?"

"My Mandarin's not as good as yours." I strapped on my waist pack, vowing never ever *ever* to remove it again.

On the other side of Gainan the truck stopped at a service shop for two hours. This annoyed Chad and Chris, but I was still flushed with relief over being aboard. Afterwards the driver and handler ran what must have been a dozen personal errands around town. As passengers we had no recourse – we'd paid our money and were along for the ride, no matter how drawn out.

When we finally resumed the road north a nasty rain crashed in, sending the handler scrambling through the window into the cab as we drove. The rest of us huddled together and lifted whatever barriers we could above our heads, burying our faces in our arms to avoid the droplets tearing in at highway speed. The truck careened left, right, left – switchbacks taken frighteningly fast on muddy roads. If we hadn't wasted more than three hours in Gainan …! But if this occurred to any of the shivering Tibetans, I couldn't tell. I admired their resilience.

We reached Xiahe around 11PM. My rear tire had blown out, so we

All headed north

Prayer leaflets in the foreground,
tents behind

Chris Orvis

Following the crowd :: Clothing
similar to Native Americans ::
Stream crossing

trudged through rain and darkness to the nearest hotel, which charged an astounding ¥150 for a room – fifteen times the cost of our prior hotel, and still the shower emitted a depressingly cold dribble. Too late for dinner, we turned in for the night hungry.

. . .

MY REAR RIM HAD BUCKLED – not surprising considering the missing spokes and hours of abuse on a truck. Before I could hunt down a bike shop, however, a commotion arose outside our window. Trucks were scurrying in to pick up Tibetans, packing them in standing room only.

We asked a woman on our hall what was happening: a Tibetan Buddhist festival, the first permitted in mainland China in thirty years. We'd stumbled into nothing less than a pilgrimage.

We locked our bikes to our bed frames, then waited outside with the throngs. A truck handler charged us three yuan each and crammed us in with more people than seemed safe. As we drove out of town I caught my first daylight view of Xiahe, a quaint city tucked in among mountains, with one golden spire presiding over a disc of shorter buildings.

Speeding back through the grasslands, we saw something that strained visual credulity.

Tents. Tens of thousands of tents: low, stark white, smothering the verdant plain. Streams of people flowed toward them from the road. A handful rode horses; a few others rode yaks or led them by bits. Men in Stetson-style hats made a striking impression against the braids and patterns of the women – a seeming marriage of the warring factions of America's Old West.

Prayer leaflets flapped white in grass and mud. Peddlers hawked fruit. Rivulets veined the grounds. A few enterprising farmers had hauled in carts as makeshift bridges; they collected one mao each to let people step over the deepest water.

We flowed with the others, ignorant of our destination but becoming aware of an epicenter ahead. The crowds stopped at an open circle as wide as a football field. In the center a tent rested on a crimson foundation, an unbroken pool of monks spilling out the sides. We worked our way to the border of the grassy divide and watched. They were listening to someone inside, someone hidden from our view but carried by distorted loudspeaker to the multitudes. I assumed the language was Tibetan.

Several police officers with electric batons patrolled the open boundary, accompanied by two or three cowboy-looking guards with bullwhips. Around us people chanted quietly, some clutching prayer wheels, others what

Crowds outside the tent ::
Monks

Chris Orvis

Curious :: Gracious host

Chris Orvis

appeared to be prayer beads. A few genuflected. Many just sat, watching as
we did.

"You are Buddhists?" asked a man about our age behind us. Behind
his black-rimmed glasses his eyes looked exhausted; he must have traveled
overnight.

"No, we're just very curious," Chris replied.

"I too am not a Buddhist. I am Muslim." He introduced himself as Hu
Peng, a 25-year-old instructor at Lanzhou University of Technology.

"So why are you here?" she asked.

"Like you, I am interested in the Buddhists. Here, take this." He offered
a postcard-size print of a blue-skinned Buddhist deity. "It is a god, a sexual
being. Do you see?" Indeed, on close inspection we *did* see: within a tangle
of limbs, streamers and flames, a masculine body enjoyed the corporeal enthusiasm of a female. Hu Peng opened his satchel to reveal a stack of similar
images. "I printed them to distribute as a blessing. The Buddhists consider
it a blessing to look at such images. Though I do not think," he chuckled
mischievously, "they are familiar with images such as these."

A midsize tanker truck ambled over the soft earth, spraying the crowds
from a turret. "It is holy water," Hu explained. "The fourth highest lama will
speak soon. He blessed the water."

"The entire truckload?" I asked, struck by this fusion of spirituality and
technology.

Guttural horns sounded. Chanting emerged from the tent; the genu-
flecting around us intensified. An oratory followed, and Hu began translating – but we didn't last long as it started raining. We fled past the worshipers,
our new friend directing us toward the deserted tents. He swung open a
canvas flap; we hesitated. "It is okay, they will not mind," he reassured.

Musty with the odor of beast and hide, the tent's interior was surprisingly
dim. Animal skins covered the grass. Sacks that I took for bedding and food
surrounded the center pole. As my eyes continued adjusting I noticed the
monk observing us. He sat silently, an elderly man with crew cut hair and a
bulbous nose. His eyes shone.

Hu Peng explained our intrusion in Tibetan; the monk responded. "He
traveled for days to this festival," Hu interpreted. "Now he is too sick to attend." A crimson arm gestured at a barrel, offering us a Tibetan staple: yak
butter. "It is good food," Hu encouraged. With the stifling smell of yak
already in our nostrils, we each feigned a taste.

We waited out the short rain in the tent, then bid farewell to our two
hosts and caught a truck back to Xiahe. From a street vendor I bought a

Circling the perimeter, touching foreheads to ash :: Manure dried for cooking fuel, with Chad in a Tibetan cowboy hat

Chris Orvis

Labrang Monastery

Chant :: Mosque prayer hall

Chris Orvis

prayer wheel for thirty yuan, plus a bag of thumb-size ceramic trinkets I planned to convert into Christmas ornaments to give away back home.

By early evening the trucks returned to town en masse. Worshipers walked the perimeter of Xiahe's monastery, touching their foreheads to walls at points marked with ash. In other places, either cow or yak manure had been packed onto the walls to dry into chips for cooking fuel. No one touched their foreheads there.

Back at the hotel we discovered a young man in our room, a college student from South Korea who'd been assigned the spare bed. A Buddhist himself, he'd heard about this festival and had traveled all the way from Seoul to attend. Thanks to his superb English we discussed Buddhism late into the night.

. . .

I FOUND A MECHANIC to fix my wheel, then poked through a music shop for cassettes of Tibetan music. Later we bumped into Hu Peng, who invited us to an outdoor restaurant for tea and bowls of rice with yak milk. During this treat we chuckled at a toddler in split pants who kept mooning us as he chased a kitten.

That afternoon Tibetan worshippers resumed circling the monastery – Labrang, the largest Buddhist monastery outside of Tibet. We joined the procession. At one point, horns droned from a courtyard across the wall. Through a wide gap in a gate we glimpsed a circle of monks rotating, arms tracing shapes in the air. People swarmed to this point to peek with us. I managed to snap one photo but stopped when the others hissed. (I didn't even know if my camera still functioned after its mountain tumble.)

Around the corner we discovered the main gate open, allowing visitors to peruse the first buildings within. One half-open door disclosed a dim, forbidding chamber of vases, statues and metal-framed mirrors. Chad and Chris tiptoed in, whispers padded in the stillness. A camera flash blasted, followed instantly by the scolding baritone of a stocky monk who seized Chris by the elbow, dragged her out, and slammed the door. Chad was still inside.

It must have been pitch black in there, and the monk kept lambasting him. "I didn't see anyone," Chris apologized, shaken. "I didn't mean to get him in trouble."

The voices within hushed. We looked at each other. "Uh, Chad?" I ventured. I wasn't about to touch the door handle.

Chad appeared from an adjacent hallway. "There was a door open on the other side," he said. "I couldn't understand him and he couldn't understand me, so I just walked out."

We decided to cool it with the cameras.

That evening we witnessed six Han Chinese police officers walking side by side down the center of Xiahe's main avenue, nightsticks in hand, expressions stern. Had something occurred somewhere in town – a bit of pro-Tibet passion? Perhaps the governing Communists had reached toleration's limit, and now felt the need to remind everyone who was in charge. Either way, the explicit show of force looked out of place, comical. Not even in Beijing had I seen such an overreaching display.

Yes, the mountains were high, the emperor distant – a hundred thousand Buddhists assembling with a ranking lama had proven that. But still, the Communist Party governed even these wild grasslands.

. . .

WE LEFT XIAHE to pedal our way up another series of rigorous ascents. Fewer Tibetan colors here; in this predominantly Muslim area people wore plain dark outfits, the men with beards, straw hats, and frameless flat-disk sunglasses I found stylish.

At an outdoor restaurant an unkempt, mumbling man descended on our table to polish off the little we hadn't eaten. He was the only person with a mental disability I noticed the entire year. The rest, I supposed, were institutionalized. Sadly, the out-of-sight, out-of-mind strategy worked: I'd practically forgotten such challenges existed.

We decided to xiuxi where a rope bridge spanned the river. The wooden slats seemed sturdy enough; only one was missing. Still, we chickened out and walked our bikes across, then laid down beneath a tree. Within minutes

Bridge :: Muslim family

Chris Orvis

a number of Muslim women and children ran over to watch, just in time for a bit of slapstick – we'd parked ourselves atop a thriving ant colony.

By late afternoon the steady sequence of villages coalesced into the outskirts of another city. Linxia dazzled us with its several-story buildings, developed stores and bona fide traffic. The hotel we found was clean, cheap at thirty yuan per night – and the rooms had TV. Civilization! Still, the water petered out midway through my shower, leaving me in suds.

Suddenly within scoring distance of Lanzhou, we realized we'd outpaced ourselves. Chris wouldn't need to catch a train for a few more days, so we kicked back in Linxia. Events leading up to the Tibetan Buddhist festival had risen to such a crescendo that our spirits couldn't help but drag afterward.

I wrote lengthy letters, mailed them home. A mosque declined us entry because Chris was wearing shorts. We watched TV: low-budget sitcoms, and Brazil beating Sweden in the World Cup semifinals.

An optician I met on the sidewalk offered to duplicate my glasses at a price I couldn't resist, so for less than $8 U.S. I picked up a backup pair. Like other opticians I'd seen, he worked out of a concrete stall next to produce and plasticware vendors, open to traffic noise and dust. Despite this dubious setup, the lenses he produced were sharp, professional, making me wonder if American optical labs were overly clinical.

One night a restaurant served us entrées that weren't exactly what we'd ordered. We chalked up the differences to local variation and dug in. Naive waiguoren! The bill rang up three times higher – the waitress had swapped our orders for more expensive alternates. With the goods already bellied, we were caught in a minor scene with the owner, who outgunned us linguistically but eventually offered to split the difference.

Health screening, Xiahe

. . .

ON THE BUS TO LANZHOU, children hopped aboard at various stops to sell snacks, drinks and newspapers. I shared a seat with a man with bandaged hands who conked out on my shoulder. A few nudges failed to rouse him, so I left him in place and took it as a sign of fitting in.

A massive city, Lanzhou reminded me of Beijing: multi-lane streets, traffic circles, buildings tall enough to require elevators. Corner vendors sold ice cream bars – pick your flavor, chocolate or banana. Unlike prior disappointments, this brand, Baishite, actually rivaled Klondike. Who knew China hid all the good ice cream out west? "We should've stayed *here* two days!" I exclaimed. I bought and consumed from three vendors in a row.

Lanzhou's luster took a hit, however, when someone stole all six bottles from our bikes while we registered for a hotel room. The railway station had no tickets east available; Chris would have to try again later. A restaurant served us slushy noodles, and afterwards the station still lacked tickets. "Guess I'm not heading out tonight after all," she sighed. "I'll just pack faster when I get back to Taiyuan." We comforted ourselves with more ice cream.

With two weeks remaining to cycle, Chad and I examined a map. "We could go anywhere from here," he said. "I've got a friend up north who would probably join us." We weighed possible routes.

I dropped my finger west, on a tiny dot in the middle of nowhere. "What's Dunhuang?"

"Part of the Silk Road. An oasis. All the rest of this," Chad indicated the empty paper around the dot, "is Gobi."

"Not bikeable, obviously."

"No, I think you can only get there by train."

Aside from the miracle of stumbling into an ice cream haven, my spirits continued to drag with post-Xiahe anticlimax. I needed something radically different to keep me going.

Dunhuang winked at us from its big blank nothing on the map.

. . .

STILL NO TICKETS EASTWARD the next day, even after waiting two hours. People were buying them out to scalp at the entrance. "And there's the police," Chris fumed, "doing nothing."

Chad and I decided against lugging our bikes and gear to Dunhuang. We paid for our hotel room four days in advance and slipped the clerk ¥50 to guarantee our possessions wouldn't be disturbed, with the promise of another

¥100 when we returned. Then we scooted our beds together so we could lock our bikes to both frames in a deterring tangle of steel. Leaving our gear behind was risky, but we didn't feel like schlepping it around unnecessarily.

On her fourth trip to the station in two days, Chris managed to score a ticket. Getting home wouldn't be quick; the journey would take her through Taiyuan, then Beijing, and finally to America. Chad and I wished her well, then bought our tickets west without issue. No glut of demand there!

At one rail stop we leaned out the window to patronize children selling instant noodles, bread and sodas – only to discover, after the train resumed rolling, that the bread was moldy. We read, chatted, played Xianqi, all the while wondering when the greenery outside would give way to desert.

That evening my stomach churned and cramped, even though I hadn't eaten the foul bread.

Must've been all that ice cream.

. . .

SUNRISE REVEALED THE DESERT LANDSCAPE that had eluded us the day before. Miserly brush dotted the crusty plain. Burnt ridges skulked in the distance. An occasional breeze lifted the otherwise still dust.

The railroad ended three hours shy of Dunhuang at a dismal outpost named Liuyuan. We would need to take a bus the rest of the way. We followed the other passengers to a squat terminal, where determination not to be stranded overnight set off a violent shoving bout that made Da Shi Tang look genteel. Wasted energy, all of it – plenty of bus seats were available.

On this final leg, the road passed low dunes, hints of oasis, and the ruins of stone walls. Students had mentioned that the Tail of the Great Wall was out here at a place called Jiayuguan; I wondered if these lesser walls were built

View from the train

around the same time period.

Dunhuang didn't quite match my vision of an oasis. Somehow I expected it to be cooler than the surrounding desert. Ha! It's difficult to describe the heat without falling into clichés. I doubted my lungs really could extract what they needed from air that temperature. Trees and colorful shops lined Dunhuang's streets, but the air itself seemed to glare in the harsh sun. Street cleaners doused the asphalt with water that evaporated within the minute; a minute later the tar would resume bubbling; a few minutes later another truck would douse the street again. If Lanzhou's specialty was ice cream, Dunhuang's was shaved ice, served with bowl and spoon since it turned to flavored water before it could be consumed.

The bus dropped us off at a hotel without vacancy, so we tromped across town (already missing our bikes) and paid for cheap dorm beds. We explored the shops along one avenue, paused to eat a small watermelon, then escaped the heat in an air-conditioned movie theater. In the film a Chinese police officer protected a woman who'd photographed a murder. Despite the cool air, we didn't stay inside long; choppy footage and an abrasive sound system propelled us out.

By 10PM the sun had begun its descent. As the temperature dropped, we realized the low level of activity we'd taken for a calm oasis had been Dunhuang's long xiuxi. At dusk people flooded the streets, sidewalks buzzing with Xianqi games, karaoke, food stalls. "Milkshake?" I read from one sign, incredulous. It turned out to be a yogurtshake.

Hocking used dong xi seemed to be the local hobby. Families spread out sheets to display clothes, kitchen utensils, old toys, then watched from their stools as couples and groups of teenagers ambled past. I couldn't help but be

Dunhuang

charmed by this pocket of humanity that scratched out a living amid a hostile desert, and thrummed late into the coolness of each night.

. . .

THROUGHOUT THE MIDDLE AGES, Buddhist monks gathered in the desert to carve their devotion into hundreds of caves cut into a rocky ridge.

A minibus drove us out for a tour of this site, Mogao Caves. Chad and I tagged onto a group led by a docent with an impeccable British accent. Each grotto's design was unique. Nearly all featured images of Buddha: painted, sculpted, two hands or many hands, with halos, with attendants, sitting, sleeping, standing, past present and future Buddhas, small Buddhas and 34-meter-tall Buddhas. Incredible artistry and labor in the middle of a wasteland – how did they manage it?

Our group passed another tour led by a guide speaking Spanish. For a minute I trailed along, fascinated to hear Spanish spoken with a Chinese accent.

Over lunch we spied an abandoned structure nestled among the shallow dunes. No road or path led its way; no signs prohibited a visit. Out we hiked, shoes slipping in the baking sand. As we approached, the structure appeared to be a plain concrete box, probably meant to house a generator but since left to crumble. Our little trek seemed a waste. Still, we pressed on, reached the open entry ... and discovered a grotto after all. Sunlight peeked through ceiling cracks, revealing a crumbled stone floor and graceful figures fading from the walls. Not too different from the other grottoes, but seeing something other people weren't made all the sweat and trouble worthwhile.

Mogao temple with 34-meter Buddha (inside) :: Near Mogao Caves

Back at the ridge we toured another section of caves, then returned to Dunhuang. A clerk at the bus terminal suggested that we take a bus the whole way back to Lanzhou, a cheap alternative we went with since we were running low on cash. The road would run straight through Jiayuguan, Tail of the Great Wall, where my students had told me a disembodied, red-headed ghost haunted a certain hotel.

Ready to hook up with his friend to the north, Chad didn't want to stop – but I couldn't pass up seeing a unique section of the Great Wall, so we planned to split up for a night. Chad would stay on the bus, and I would rejoin him in Lanzhou after a night in Jiayuguan.

During dinner, severe stomach pains prevented me from eating. I held my gut the whole way back to the hotel and moaned in bed. I'd already endured a year of digestive issues ranging from everyday rumbling to periodic all-out evacuative crises – but this pain, sharp and demanding, felt different. It took all my concentration to make it from one moment to the next.

When Chad showed up around sundown, my condition caught him off guard. "I don't think this is something I ate," I grunted. "It's just in one place, really sharp and stabbing." Then, after a moment: "Where's my appendix?"

"Come on," he said, skeptical. "If it's that bad, let's find you a hospital."

Memories of red tape trouble at a Beijing hospital, plus a fear of unclean needles, unnerved me. "No, I think I'll just die right here."

Later, the pain only intensifying and confirming my fears, I wrote down my mother's telephone number. "Tell her the trip was worth it, that I don't regret a thing."

Chad laughed – "You're not dying, moron" – but he sounded concerned. I would feel bad leaving him to deal with my remains, half a globe away from family and within an infrastructure he didn't understand. Were our roles reversed, I wouldn't know where to begin. But Chad, the older, more experienced traveler, was Type A, resourceful; he'd figure it out. Besides, it wasn't really up to me. Well, the hospital part was, but if a Beijing hospital had made me nervous I wasn't about to find out what passed for medical care after hours in the desert.

Soon enough Chad fell asleep, leaving me to fiddle with his shortwave radio until I found some soothing Indian-style music – a calming backdrop for my final hours.

. . .

DAYLIGHT THWARTED THE WINDOW SHADE. Children's high-pitched glee erupted through the wall. Chad still lay across the room. Evidently I'd slept the night, had even beaten him awake – with no trace of abdominal pain.

What was *that* about?

We boarded the bus for the long haul back to Lanzhou. Whatever dramatic adventure I expected from a 24-hour non-air conditioned drive through the Gobi quickly fizzled into a flat, hot nothingness punctuated by one meal stop and infrequent pee breaks. Four drivers rotated every few hours at the wheel. One entertained himself by barking at passengers and his fellow drivers for any reason his crimped mind could invent; the rest of us glazed over the dullness out the windows.

As the hours crept by, I read from a book of translated Tibetan Buddhist scriptures I'd picked up in Dunhuang. In one story a prince threw his body off a cliff to feed a family of starving wolves too weak to kill him themselves. Another had a king cut a thousand holes in his own body to light a thousand candles in them. Another king fed his wife and son to a hungry demon, then offered his own body in exchange for wisdom. Such extreme examples of self-negation struck me as completely foreign to the mindset of my own culture.

Yet I began contemplating a little self-negation of my own: leaving the trip early. We'd set aside almost two more weeks for travel, but where we would go and why eluded me. Meeting up with Chad's friend to cycle through a predominantly Muslim region didn't interest me nearly as much as the traveling we'd already done. Besides, stuffing my eyeballs with more sights felt gluttonous. It had been over a year since I'd left everyone I knew in America. Lacking a compelling reason to delay my return, I felt twelve months of homesickness caving in.

Nevertheless, at the stop in Jiayuguan I stood dutifully, backpack in hand. Plans were plans. "See you at the hotel in Lanzhou," I said. "Sure you don't want to come? Tail of the Great Wall?"

Speeding through the Gobi

209

"I think I'll pass."

"Once in a lifetime chance to see it."

Chad sort of snorted as he pointed out the window. "You can see it right there."

I'd been visualizing a Great Wall as impressive as the one I knew a thousand miles away. The ridiculousness of this notion struck me the moment my eyes fell on the stubby, eroded mound that paralleled our road, no different from the sad chunks of wall we'd seen on the train ride out. In disbelief I asked one of the drivers, "Na shi shen me (*What is that*)?"

"Chang Cheng (*Great Wall*)," he answered.

So much for the Wall; what about Jiayuguan itself? I scanned the town – dust-ridden as a moisture farm on Tatooine. "I'll consider it seen," I told Chad, and paid the drivers for the remainder of the trip. It felt good to push on even the slightest bit closer to home.

Our bus broke down twice that afternoon. To escape the broiling metal roof we squatted in the sun, the road silent as three drivers tinkered with, and one cursed, the engine. The desert's lack of privacy made potty breaks amusing: one merely trotted out a respectable enough distance to conduct one's business in the diminutive yet plain sight of all others.

At dusk the moon hung in the sky like a subtle ornament. Later it dipped near the horizon, where it cast a glow across the sandy terrain until it, too, joined the sun in hiding, leaving us hurtling through a black void beneath a canopy of stars.

. . .

AT FOUR IN THE MORNING we parked at an unmarked building. The drivers knocked to wake the proprietor. Breakfast. Nobody minded the lofty prices – we'd had just one opportunity for a meal the day before.

Approaching sunrise we entered a green valley, making me expect Lan-

Broken down

zhou's outskirts any moment. I'd forgotten the hours it took, going out, to reach the desert. Our bus began to pick up and drop off short-term riders, making this last stretch seemed interminable. Around noon we arrived in Lanzhou, after 26½ hours aboard.

At the hotel we discovered our gear packed so poorly the saddlebags wouldn't buckle. Someone had rifled through it. A quick inventory turned up nothing missing, so we decided not to make a stink about it; we would simply switch to another hotel, preferably one cheaper than the ¥60 per night we'd been paying.

Surprise, surprise: the hotel clerk made his own stink. We'd promised him ¥100 to keep our gear safe, but now he claimed the deal was for ¥100 *each*. Did he suppose we'd never seen that trick? We dropped two fifties on the counter and walked out.

After setting up in a dorm-style hotel, we stopped by Lanzhou University of Technology to look up Hu Peng, our Muslim friend from the Xiahe festival. He wasn't in – one more misfire in what seemed a recent spate of misfires. I felt directionless.

Over noodles I broached the possibility of me returning to America early. "I'll keep going until we hook up with your friend," I told Chad. "I won't leave you on your own."

"That's ridiculous," he answered. "It'd take you a week out of the way, and you'd have to come right back here for a train. Why not just leave from here?" Chad assured me he'd be fine; he even felt he could use the time alone to sort through plans for his future in the States. I suspected he might appreciate not having me tugging in other directions. After all, he *was* stuck with the chaperone.

I'd hoped to be released after one more week of cycling, but by the time we paid for our noodles it was settled: I would head back to Beijing the very next morning. This agreement infused me with a new rush of energy.

One of the beds in our dorm room had been taken by a British traveler named Richard. Recently divorced, he'd cashed in a business stake so he could cycle around the world. Richard had started in Tokyo and crossed Japan, flown to South Korea and crossed that peninsula, then flown and cycled from Tianjin to Beijing to Xian to Lanzhou, to continue on from there. All on bike. He'd set aside one year for the journey but had no pressing matters requiring him home if it took longer. My mind boggled at his tenacity – what he'd already accomplished made our little trip sound feeble.

More power to you, I thought, listening to his conquests and dreams. You can pedal the whole world, but I'm done hauling my carcass from one point to the next. Dropping out of the expedition felt premature, even a tad disappointing, but I couldn't wait to rejoin my family and friends.

Time to go home.

. . .

A SERIES OF OBSTACLES LOOMED between me and America, first among them the Lanzhou railway station. I hoped a sunrise start would make a difference, but scalpers already were emerging from the crowded windows with dozens of tickets in hand. Fortunately, by the time I pushed through to the windows, the pricier soft sleeper tickets were still available.

The train to Xian wouldn't depart until afternoon, so I made a few phone calls about bumping my flight forward. "Not possible," reported one service rep. He invited me to purchase a new ticket for ¥8,000. Ouch!

Sixteen hours by rail to Xian: sixteen measly hours to undo weeks of pedaling and hitchhiking and buses. I played cards with the three Chinese Air Force officers in my cabin; they shared with me a meal of bread and fermented cabbage. When our conversation tapered off I indulged in some cultural dissonance by reading a copy of Dickens' *A Tale of Two Cities* I'd found in a Lanzhou bookstore. Between chapters I wondered if I'd made the right decision. Chad would be all right, no doubt about that – but suppose I couldn't change my ticket and ended up stuck in Beijing? A midnight thunderstorm washed away these worries, lulling me to sleep.

From the platform in Xian I walked straight to the ticket windows and waited five and a half hours to buy a ticket to Beijing. With the rest of the day to kill in town, I caught up with Eliza at Dad's Home Cooking (Mum's had already replicated their new sign), then joined Eric for dinner at the Sheraton. On the overnight to Beijing I swapped stories with two American girls, both

Toddlers at Dad's Home Cooking

literature majors on a summer excursion.

After all that adventuring, you'd think home turf would be easy – but leaving the Beijing station I got turned around, asked a pedestrian which way was north, and spent twenty minutes pedaling south thanks to his little joke. This one was no language goof: *bei*, the first syllable of *Beijing*, was easy enough to understand; so was *nan*, used in *Nanjing* ("south capital," a historic reference). I imagine he enjoyed telling his friends about the clueless tourist he'd sent on a wild dragon chase.

With Lin Da's campus shut down I couldn't reach my waiban – déjà vu – and still had no luck changing my flight over the phone. Thankfully Mom, working the airline from her end in America, succeeded, giving me two days to pack.

As I sifted through my possessions, deciding what to bring and what to bequeath, a live-action adaptation of Xi You Ji (*Journey to the West*) aired on TV. One of China's literary masterpieces, it chronicled a monk and his three bodyguards, including the famous Monkey King, on a westward pilgrimage to bring Buddhist scriptures back to China. I'd encountered a few incarnations of this tale throughout the year and couldn't help chuckling at its appearance now, right as I'd completed one journey west and was about to embark on another.

A month ago I could have been right here, I thought, packing my bags. How close I'd come to making the easy choice – I would've gone home believing I'd seen China! Granted, through two semesters in Beijing I'd developed culture-spanning friendships. But then, like the hyperspace climax of Kubrick's *2001: A Space Odyssey*, a glimpse of China's full color and diversity exploded before my eyes – terraces and rockslides, grasslands and dunes, tents and prayer wheels and rope bridges and threshing wheat.

My most vivid impressions were of people, and as I flipped through my journal I found myself returning to entries from the first days out west. Eliza and her home-cooking father. The woman calling "Mianzibao!" down a bleary street. The young man who improved my rock-skipping throw, and the shy, Da Bai Tu-loving girl who hid behind younger children.

I would never see them again.

I'd almost never met them at all.

How magical, those first steps of flinging myself into the Anything Else that awaited.

. . .

I'd promised Johnny a visit before flying home. Back on my old clunker,

I pedaled with guitar case in hand – a precarious enough maneuver that I stayed in step with the other traffic. All year I'd observed bicyclists managing unwieldy cargo; now I joined them, melting into the scene, just one more figure in the snow globe. It was relaxing. Why hadn't I biked this way all year?

The guitar surprised Johnny. "Oh, you are going to play us some music?"

"Nope." I lifted it into both hands and extended it to him. "This is a gift."

"Oh, no," he laughed nervously, "this is yours. I must not take it."

"I can't take it back to America. I'm already taking my bike – I can't take the guitar too. I want it to be yours." It took considerable coaxing, but he relented.

Over dinner Johnny's parents asked for stories about my trip. As I described in terms Johnny could translate, it struck me that I was telling them about their own country. I'd seen areas of China they had not, perhaps never would. Some Americans never leave their home state; at that point I still hadn't visited several regions of my own country, and could imagine being fascinated by a foreign tourist's tales. The primary issue was to Go. I wondered how much Not Going, both in China and America, was influenced by economics, culture, and plain old personality.

After the meal and some television, I rose to leave. Johnny's family balked. "The news says it will rain very badly. You must stay a while."

"It's just twenty minutes home. I'll make great time without the guitar."

"What if you do not make it? You will get very wet I think."

"I can make it. I'll go fast." This conversation dragged on, Johnny translating his parents' objections and me digging in my American heels. Still not finished packing, the thought of watching more TV panicked me. What was a little weather? I could beat it.

Muttering the entire way about black clouds, Johnny walked me to the foyer. He removed his wristwatch and presented it to me in both hands. "I want you to have this. As a goodbye gift."

"I can't take your watch!"

"You must have." He pressed it into my palm. "It will help you in your travels." This was silly – I already had a watch. His was nice, too: brassy finish, classic face. I really didn't want to take it from him.

Still, the resolve in his face was clear. I'd given him my guitar out of practicality, but this exchange created a guanxi imbalance. A lack of reciprocation would be a breach of friendship. After all we'd been through, Johnny was absolutely determined not to part that way.

I replaced my watch with his and admired it with gratitude.

This interchange extended our farewell long enough that by the time I turned the corner and got my bearings, I regretted leaving. A black stormpot of clouds leered. I would be drenched for sure unless I hustled like never before, working my flopping pedals like a maniac.

Other bicyclists abandoned the streets to shrink beneath store awnings. I cranked past them furiously.

Fifteen minutes from home, the first drops fell.

Then the air turned liquid.

The sheer mass that slammed down soaked me through in an instant. Taxis jerked to the curb; people fled the awnings for store interiors. Stunned by the blast, I veered to the sidewalk and took refuge under the first awning I could reach, panting and dripping on the wrong side of a window of staring people. Funny Lao Wai! Didn't it rain in America?

I'd seen only a few rains in Beijing – certainly nothing like this sustained volume crashing down every incredible second. Never would I have expected such a storm so close to the Gobi. The warm asphalt produced a steam that obscured stores across the street.

As for the street itself, I stood there, doused and muggy, marveling at a Beijing street perfectly … empty.

The monsoon had to subside any minute. No way could such intensity be sustained. After five minutes of people staring at me, though, I changed my mind. What was the point of waiting? I was already soaked. Home was a mere fifteen minutes away, and the world had been transformed.

Setting off expressions of amazement on the curtain of faces behind the glass, I mounted my bicycle and headed out.

As a toddler I had feared showers, convinced it was impossible to breathe within rushing water. This sensation triggered that old emotion. It was ludicrously wet, deliriously wet, like biking along the bottom of a lake. I weaved in lazy curves down the center of the street, cackling, hooting. Through the downpour I could make out gray figures ogling the lone idiot who'd lost his mind. I doubted they could tell I was a waiguoren, and it tickled me to think they were seeing one of their own spurning the crowd, spurning nature itself.

A few hours earlier I'd prided myself on blending in, pacing everyone else. Now I was the sole nincompoop in the rain, the rest of Beijing watching, motionless as I passed. I crooned until I was hoarse for the sheer joy of competing against, and losing to, the thunderous roar.

Conforming to the culture around me had been fun. But I was still American, and found more thrill shouting into the storm.

Long Corridor, Yihe Yuan

Epilogue

Before heading to the airport I crammed my pockets with toilet paper, then stuffed a backup roll in my carry-on. It would be a long flight. Only when I entered the plane's restroom did I realize my silliness. How a year had conditioned me!

In Seattle-Tacoma I beheld a glorious sight – Dunkin' Donuts – only to enter a dilemma: thirty-five cents for a donut. Was that expensive? Attempting to resurrect my sense of U.S. currency, I jiggled a quarter and dime in my palm. Airports were notorious for high prices. I trusted this truism and pocketed the coins.

Signs in English, conversations in English, PA announcements in English! I almost missed the hush of illiteracy, even as I basked in gestures and habits that came naturally.

This hand-in-glove cultural match flooded me with confidence as I re-settled in Baltimore. I was precisely where I was supposed to be. Each decision I made – housing, employment, dating – shone with a golden luster. Everything smacked of rosy-colored rightness.

Simultaneously, the littlest change felt wrong, like the post office. "Would you like self-adhesives?" asked the postal clerk.

"What? No!" I blurted, frowning at the booklet she proffered. Then, squinting: "What is it?"

"Like stickers," she explained, taken aback by my ignorance. "Look." She pantomimed using the new stamp, then handed me the booklet.

I passed it back. "No, I want the same stamps I've always had." Those behind me marveled at the 23-year-old geezer. After leaving a nation where stamps and glue were separate products, I was all hot and bothered over self-adhesives? Something about reverse culture shock made me fervent to find home exactly the way I'd left it.

What struck me most upon returning? The combativeness of our national discourse. Liberal! Conservative! Democrat! Republican! Every news story yanked between two sides of a locked-horn ideological war. Our media seemed intent on splitting our brains. Could a healthy mind survive such a climate? In China I'd asked just such a question about the numbing deception of single party concord, only to wonder if America's cognitive hostility was any healthier. Yes, our marketplace of ideas is necessary, precious and free; I just never realized how equally discordant and ugly it can be until I left it for a year.

Yet I contributed to that ugliness myself – and discovered how profoundly Communism had upset me – when I met, at a farmer's market in the Charles Village neighborhood of Baltimore, a man distributing free issues of the Communist Party USA newspaper. My feet stopped cold.

"Here, take an issue," he said, paper extended.

"Are you kidding? I just got back from *China*." I leveled the words at him loudly, a public rebuke.

"Oh, then you know firsthand," he rejoined good-naturedly, accepting my invitation to create an audience, "what a fine job the CPC is doing to make China the world's next leader." Unshaven, mid-thirties, lightly balding and in his slippers, he'd looked only partially awake until I'd roused him.

"I know what my students' lives were like," I spat. "Communism was rammed down their throats. The newspapers were pure propaganda. They

*At a restaurant
in the mountains
near Diebu*

Chris Orvis

218

couldn't even call long distance without registering, and they were all desperate to come to America. Why do you think that is?"

He responded in the same affable way, assuring me that I had misunderstood, that my students were in fact flourishing – in contrast to the millions suffering in poverty in America. This was in fact the most prosperous age China had ever known …

People cleared space around us, watching, and the argument was slipping away. Some of what I'd said sounded oversimplified and out of context, whereas some of what he was saying made sense. And who was the one losing his cool? It was all coming across wrong, so I went for the jugular: "Listen, have you even *heard* of the Cultural Revolution?"

"The Cultural Revolution was the best thing that ever happened to China!"

I don't remember what I said after that. I do know that it was yelled. I also recall my feet stepping forward, and his back. Eyes around us widened – I'd completely lost it. I waved him off and stormed away.

Calm down. Calm *down*. I forced myself to take deeper breaths. What was my problem? Something about my students' situation had gotten to me. It wasn't that they were Capital-O Oppressed; they weren't. Neither were they necessarily Disenfranchised or even Underprivileged. I didn't know if capitalism and democracy had all the answers, or even the best answers. Who knew what the answers were?

Yet I'd heard my students' hushed tones when they discussed Tiananmen Square. I'd read their compositions, some of them filled with angst, others hungry for ideas from the outside. They distrusted their own media. They suspected the record of their nation's history wasn't accurate. They seemed to

Free Talk

regard their own futures with a sense of fate instead of choice.

Within a political machine that ascribed to itself all truth, it was only natural that they should weigh any lingering dissatisfactions against their own Party. By raising the bar so high, Communism consequently fell so far.

Still, my students negotiated a living out of life, just as I would in America. Conditions are conditions. We all cultivate our gardens, gleaning what spirit and laughter we can along the way.

And I *did* believe in the marketplace of ideas, even if an American Communist didn't.

I walked back to the farmer's market an hour later. He was still there. His eyes popped on seeing me, but I approached with my face open and palms up. "I'm sorry about earlier," I said. "That was wrong of me. This is America, and you've got a right to your opinions. I'm sorry."

He wasn't prepared for this. In the awkward moment that followed, for lack of anything better to say, he mumbled, "You want a newspaper?"

I laughed. "I said I was sorry," I answered, "but not that sorry."

. . .

IN 2001 BEIJING RE-BID FOR THE OLYMPICS and won. How I wish I could have seen my students' faces when they heard the announcement!

In the summer of 2006 my sister-in-law taught English in Beijing, with the Olympics just twenty months away. "Could you feel it?" I asked when Kelly returned. "How are the preparations going?"

"Everywhere you look there's construction, cranes," she reported. "And the government's trying to teach people to stand in lines."

I smiled. "How's that going?"

Karaoke party

Kelly shrugged. "They're trying *really* hard. The bus stops have these little fences to keep people in line, and a woman stands there with a flag to help them cue up. But there's only so much you can change about human behavior in such a short time." After a moment she added, "Oh, and people still spit."

Would Beijing pull it off? I was skeptical – an attitude only reinforced by reports of smoggy air, facades built to hide older areas, and indications that the Communist Party might forbid live telecasts. Even Bird's Nest Stadium looked as though it was trying too hard to impress.

But watching the opening ceremony – danced calligraphy on an immense video scroll, thousands of neon percussionists, video globe with runners along the latitudes – I was impressed. Genuinely, deeply impressed. Scale, artistry, innovation, coordination, vision: they'd delivered the whole package.

In retrospect, the earlier slogan, "A More Open China Awaits Olympics 2000," sounds ingratiating. A Millennium Beijing Olympics would have paled next to what we saw in 2008. To their credit, China's leaders had swallowed the bitter pill of rejection, accepting and even embracing the truth that impressing the world would take more work. Consequently, by 2008 China was not merely "more open" – she had pulled out every stop with spectacles the world had never seen. It was inspiring.

That's not to suggest the Olympics went off without a hitch. There was that matter of computer-simulated fireworks between Tiananmen Square and Bird's Nest Stadium. And that other matter about one girl lip-syncing to a different girl's voice. "Phony!" Western media cried.

Surely our reaction puzzled the Chinese. "We went the extra mile for you," they must have thought. "We invested in state-of-the-art graphics to make the fireworks look perfect. We conducted a nationwide search to match the perfect face with the perfect voice. Why would you complain about the extra care we took to honor you?"

I never heard this perspective mentioned in our media. The cultural divide persists.

. . .

PEOPLE ASK IF I'M STILL IN TOUCH with my students. During that first year back I mailed off a few letters, but who knows if I addressed them correctly. In 1996 Johnny snail-mailed his email address to my mother, and for two years we wrote occasionally. But computers crash, ISPs change (this was before webmail), and mothers move; I haven't heard from him since. The last I knew, Johnny still hoped to enter a graduate program in America. I don't know if his dream came true.

The only other student I've ever heard from was Rebecca, one of the Free Talk regulars. In 1998 I received an email from her out of the blue – she was in Chicago for a one-month training program. She'd found one of my old websites and invited me to visit. Simple hospitality dictated that I fly out; she was, after all, meeting me nine-tenths of the way. Unfortunately my tight private school salary was being depleted by car troubles; I couldn't afford a ticket. Since Rebecca didn't have email in China, we also fell out of touch.

I've tried searching the Internet for my students, but I'm still functionally illiterate when it comes to Chinese characters and have trouble navigating the results. They're out there, their language skills are better than mine, and the Internet's reach continues to grow. It's only a matter of time.

The other question people ask is whether I will return. Already Beijing is strikingly different from the Beijing I knew: electric bicycles, cell phones and the Internet, booming private businesses, colorful high-rise behemoths, and an economic might that year by year turns my own country into a debtor. In 2009 we learned that China's automobile market has outgrown our own, and that China is now second only to the U.S. in number of billionaires.

Google Earth shows that my apartment building has been razed, as has the building where I taught and the xia hai store where I bought snacks for Free Talks. Xizhimen, the swarming intersection with a separate circle for bicycle traffic, now looks like a highway interchange that doesn't even support bicycles (do they pass through tunnels?). Most amazing to me, everything I knew in my proving grounds, Wudaokou market, is gone – stamped out by

Wudaokou market no longer exists

a bulky high-rise.

All of this aggressive economic change has occurred, oddly enough, beneath a single immovable constant: one-party rule. The promise of a "socialist market economy with Chinese characteristics" has indeed fueled cities in their catch-up pursuit of prosperity, giving birth to a chimaera: an Information Age society with state-controlled media and filtered Internet. When even a "Don't Be Evil" corporation like Google bends its knee to Communist censors, it's doubtful that the Chinese will enjoy full freedom of expression anytime soon. The Communist Party has wrought much good in recent years, but like all political parties, its chief end is still itself.

Whether or not I do return, China will always play a role in my life. I haven't kicked the habit of saying "No no no no no," an English version of "Bu bu bu bu bu." I recognize snatches of Mandarin from passersby at the mall. Because most of my language learning occurred in real situations, Mandarin phrases sometimes percolate in my dreams. And when my sons announce it's time to get going they shout, "Zou ba!"

Sensitivity to cross-cultural experiences inspired my wife and I to host a foreign exchange student. I helped launch a high school Chinese program by recruiting students (pretty easy when you tell them the verbs aren't conjugated). Face and guanxi continue to influence the way I relate to others, and music from other countries still captivates me.

Occasionally I stumble across video footage from China and recognize certain tidbits: a gesture or facial expression; a style of stage setting; the bored twitch of a security guard, or the gentle maneuvering of bicycles. In many ways that year has telescoped into a distant dream … but it was also long, and Beijing a place I *inhabited*. Which means that for all my feeling out of place, China still became a part of me.

So when I come across these familiar flashes from halfway around the world, confound it all if my sense of nostalgia doesn't feel a little bit like home.

WHAT ARE YOU DOING, Dad?"

"I'm writing."

"Can I watch?"

"Well, it's not … oh, why not."

After a few seconds, leaning into the screen: "Are you writing your book?"

"Yes."

"*The Year I Smelled Like Milk*?"

"Yes."

"Why did you smell like milk?"

I'd mentioned the title a few days earlier but hadn't bothered to explain. The kid was three. Now, though, he was asking directly, so I gave it a try. I took it slowly, step by step. Smelling like milk was a matter of perspective, and maybe that was so basic, so foundational to human experience, that even a three-year-old could understand.

My son nodded the whole way through. Did he really get it?

I think so, because after a minute he said, "Maybe when I grow up, I'll go to China."

"That'd be cool. You'll learn a lot."

"Will I smell like milk, too?"

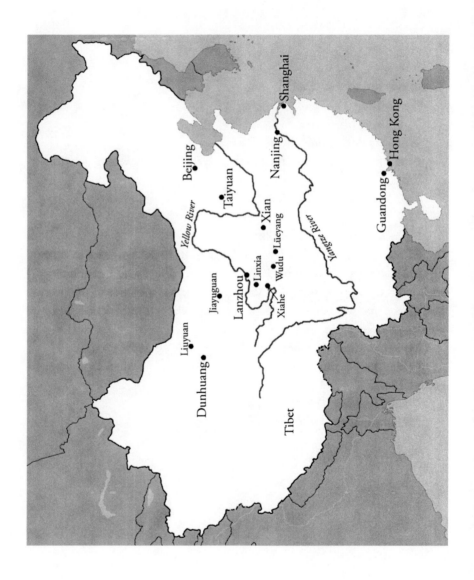

Notes

二百二十七

IMAGES: Unless otherwise noted, I took all photographs in 1993 and 1994 using a point-and-shoot camera (Canon Snappy Q) and local film processors in Beijing. Some images were scanned from realia I brought home from China in 1994. Cycling partner (and superior photographer) Chris Orvis has graciously permitted me to include many of her photographs in the chapter "Journey to the West."

Names: The names of all Chinese citizens, including their English classroom names, have been changed.

Compositions: Sixteen students gave me permission to publish anonymous selections from their writing. Little did I suspect it would take fifteen years for my own thoughts to coalesce into this project. I'm delighted to share, at long last, their voices with a wider audience. I've kept the original grammar intact to preserve the flavor of their writing. If these compositions read awkwardly, kindly consider that I would be stretched to compose even ten consecutive words in Chinese. My students' language skills far exceeded my own.

Dialogue: I've incorporated grammatical variances common among the English learners I knew in Beijing in order to convey the feel of conversation. No disrespect is intended.

Page 14, Olympics: I've found the European feed on the Internet, but not footage of Beijing's reaction. Someone in China is bound to have recorded it on videocassette. It'll surface on the Internet eventually.

Page 20, accent: Chinese English had a British influence, due in part to Great Britain's colonization (make that *colonisation*) of Hong Kong. I was a bit concerned when students kept calling me a "naughty young man" – what was I doing wrong? – until finally I asked, and they explained *naughty* as clever and mischievous. Evidently some British flavoring there.

Pages 26-27, market economy: I was fascinated to see the capital of the world's largest Communist nation rename streets and bridges after the highest bidder – typically corporations.

Page 47, university majors: One grad student, Peggy, told me her specialty was particle board technology. I blinked, prompting an explanation: a particle board technologist researched the entire manufacturing process in order to develop stronger and more specialized construction materials.

Peggy wore pigtails and bangs; she was so shy she poked out her tongue in a sort of silent squeak whenever I looked at her in class. Particle board technology? "You like this?" I asked.

"It is quite special," she answered, her spine straightening. "I am the only graduate student doing this. There is only one professor. He is old, so I work closely with him to learn everything. I was lucky to be chosen."

"But do you *like* it?"

She half-shrugged. "It is okay. Some parts are interesting." This came in a tone of near surprise. Then she added, "It is just strange to spend every day in the lab with one man." No kidding – whenever I saw Peggy she was in giggling lockstep with other girls. I couldn't imagine a more unexpected person to receive the mantle of China's leading particle board technologist.

Page 50, badminton: I considered badminton a whimsy until I saw a Lin Da tournament. Matches were fast-paced and every bit as aggressive as professional table tennis. Search the Internet for videos of professional badminton and you'll see what I mean.

Page 50, purchasing card: I received a small jolt of surprise when my colleague Augustina Menegay translated the directions for me, 15 years later:

1. Keep this ID card safe. Exchange it for a new one when completely used.

Bicycle parking

A fine will be imposed if the card is lost.
2. *This card is not transferable. It is invalid if altered. Return the card before leaving the university.*
3. *Valid only after stamped.*

I had no idea I was supposed to return this card to Lin Da.

Page 54, Coke: The transliteration of *Coca-Cola* into *Ke Kou Ke Le* 可口可乐 ("Delicious Happiness") was considered a monumental success.

Page 61, ching chong: Rosie O'Donnell's "humor" on ABC's *The View*, broadcast December 5, 2006, offended Asians around the world.

Page 62, powdered milk: When I showed my colleague Augustina Menegay the packaging of my favorite brand of naifen, she translated a second line that identified it as infant formula.

Page 65, toilet paper: Years later a major U.S. brand began advertising ridged paper as a great innovation. "Big deal," I thought, "the Chinese have been using that for decades!"

Page 67, tai chi: An online reviewer pointed out that men do practice tai chi, and that some tai chi movements are quick in tempo. Duly noted. I've presented only the unusual gender characterization my students used when explaining tai chi to me.

Page 68, Party unity: This quote appeared in "Jiang Calls for Deep Study of Deng Book," published November 3, 1993 in *China Daily*, page 1.

Page 71, tones: Superstition surrounded the number four. In Mandarin this number was *si*, spoken with the falling fourth tone – but the same syllable

Children on the street to Wudaokou

spoken with the bouncing third tone meant "die."

Page 71, shortcuts: I also charged my students with ignoring the stroke order of written characters – their handwriting looked to me like goofy scribbles. They explained that the loops and curls of their sloppy writing still followed the essence of each character's strokes, only without lifting the pen – roughly parallel to writing English in cursive.

Page 71, alphabet: Unlike our own alphabet, the Chinese oral alphabet made sequential sense. If you pronounce the syllables and pay attention to the movements of your mouth, you'll feel them following an oral geography:

bo po mo fo | *de te ne le* | *ge ke he* | *ji qi xi* | *zhi chi shi* | *ri zi ci si*

Compare this to our ABC's – how are *they* organized?

Page 72, dyslexia: For more on the connection between dyslexia and irregular spellings, search the Internet using the terms *dyslexia* and *different orthographies* (writing systems).

Page 74, counting: The Chinese hand signs for numbers resembled some American Sign Language signs:

    6 – similar to Y
    7 – similar to E, but with fingers and thumb extended outward
    8 – similar to L
    9 – similar to X
    10 – similar to A

Page 79, sparrows: Students told me the exterminated birds were *pigeons*. An online reviewer informed me they were actually sparrows, which is verified easily online.

Carving jack-o'-lanterns

The *New York Times* article "From Pest to Meal: A Leap Forward?" by Chris Buckley, published April 3, 2002, described a unique method for dispatching sparrows:

In the late 1950's, when Mao began his assault on sparrows, he lumped them together with rats, mosquitoes and flies as the "four pests" to be killed off.

Millions of citizens were mobilized to clang pots and pans until frightened birds dropped to the ground in exhaustion and were beaten to death. Up to 18 million birds were killed before scientists persuaded Mao to replace the sparrow with the bedbug on his list.

Page 79, spitting: "Beijing Clamps Down on Spitting," written by Rupert Wingfield-Hayes, appeared March 1, 2006 on the *BBC News* website. From the article:

Foreign visitors to Beijing are often astonished by its citizens' capacity for expelling mucus. Spitting is not just confined to the open air. The floors of shops and restaurants are often peppered with phlegm. But Beijingers are now being told they must abandon this cherished tradition.

Page 83, whistle band: One day his bird may even haunt the sky above a young waiguoren, who will say to his companions, "There, that noise! I hear it every few weeks – it sounds like a UFO. What *is* that?"

Page 89, post office: Many students collected stamps, including American stamps. Knowing this, my mother sent me packages with as many small denomination stamps as would fit. I distributed them to students as rewards.

Page 95, BICF: Quote from the Beijing International Christian Fellowship website, www.bicf.org.

Four smiles

Page 99, Pizza Hut: Lactose intolerance ruined Johnny's Pizza Hut experience – he suffered terrible cramps from the pizza cheese. I don't recall Pizza Hut being very popular in Beijing, presumably for this reason. Kentucky Fried Chicken, on the other hand, was an immense hit, despite the Chinese reluctance to eat with their hands. I bicycled past the KFC near Bei Da several times, and often saw the customer line extending out the doors.

Pages 101-102, outsider: Prior cross-cultural experiences didn't quite prepare me for immersive isolation. I spent three years as a haole in Hawaii, three years as a gringo in Puerto Rico, and a summer as a muzungu in Uganda. Yet during these periods I was accompanied by others (family, friends, classmates) of my own ethnicity. Even in Beijing I lived with other American teachers. Without these exceptions, the full impact of immersion weighed in.

Page 105, Xiangqi: A few more rules. Close guards weren't allowed to leave the palace, and could move only diagonally. Elephants weren't allowed to cross the river. Soldiers (pawns) captured forward, not diagonally, and became more powerful after they crossed the river, able to move and attack sideways as well. Horses and elephants didn't "jump" over pieces, which meant their movements could be blocked. Because cannons could attack only *over* an intervening piece, a common defense was to move the intervening piece *out of the way* – quite counterintuitive.

Page 116, train: A scan of my unused ticket to Taiyuan is on page 11.

Pages 117-118, firecrackers: Quotations are from the *China Daily* commentary "Season's Greetings" published February 9, 1994, page 4. It included this conciliatory nod:
  However, we also hope the absence of firecrackers will have no effect on the

Waiting for the bus with Joan

fun of the festival, as events and festivities are to be even more appealing and varied than in previous years.
Beijing lifted the ban on firecrackers twelve years later.

Page 128, grading: Don't use red ink for grading homework! The Chinese wrote in red to break off a relationship.

Page 141, pickpocket: Comment from one reviewer regarding this confrontation: "In the U.S. we'd worry about weapons or a possible fight. Culture changes everything." True enough – concern about my personal safety didn't even occur to me.

Page 157, song: Translation of the refrain of "Xiao Fang":
Thank you for giving me love
Love I will never forget
Thank you for giving me your heart
Your heart will always be with me

Page 159, inner tubes: I packed my Diamondback and brought it to America as checked luggage. A month later, someone in Baltimore stole the foot-pump beneath my seat, necessitating that I change the inner tubes and throw out all my spares. The thief didn't understand that a Chinese pump wouldn't fit any American valve.

Page 160, apartment: One student's description of a family apartment:
In China, most of the people are living in apartment, and people don't want to live very far from their workplace because of the terrible traffic. If you and your family live together in a three-rooms apartment in the city, you will be always dreamed of a house with its own playground, but it's just a dream.

Forbidden City

Page 169, Dad's: *Lonely Planet* and other travel resources still list Dad's Home Cooking as a must-stop for backpackers in Xian.

Page 171, mianzibao: I assumed *mianzibao* meant "newspaper," but I've been unable to obtain a translation. Was it the title of a specific publication?

Page 178, close call: Our near collision with the elderly woman was the first memory Chris recalled when she and I spoke over the phone for the first time in fifteen years. Later, after reviewing this chapter, she wrote, "Wow, this memory was so much more life changing for me than for you. It was *the* most terrifying experience of my life." Chris believed it was physically impossible for her to miss the woman, and credits divine intervention for the averted disaster.

Page 183, lunch: Description of a lunch stop from a student composition:
> *Many years ago, my whole family was moving to the Yunnan Province, south-west China. After 3 days and nights by train, we were taken by truck to go through mountains. During that 3 days our driver was often stopped in front of a small house and eat something. Such small houses were always very dark and dirty, the food there was expensive.*

Page 199, monk: Inspired by our tent host, I wrote the following piece of fiction in 2002:
> *The first pilgrimage in mainland China in decades – but he wouldn't go. It was too far, his bones creaked, he hadn't left the monastery in ages, and didn't he feel a little sick? He could learn nothing from a Lama that he didn't already know from the grottoes and flags and prayer wheels of his home.*
>
> *They escorted him by the elbows, lifted him into the open bed of the truck. Knee to knee, forty-two red robes huddled in the light blue box – he*

Always a comedian

counted them often, and grinned when tight turns mashed them all together. Down from the mountains, where the air warmed, it rained in pounding fists; his brothers could not keep him dry. They felt guilty at the ritual grounds when, wracked by chills, he stayed behind in the tent.

They would feel even guiltier later, discovering his vacant remains. But that was because they didn't understand what he'd seen: valleys sweeping beneath hairpin roads; tents strewn like prayer sheets tousled in the wind; a fair-skinned Western woman that made him blush like a schoolboy; a ruddy toddler hawking newspapers with a resonant, reaching call; where the driver tinkered with the engine, a fallen eagle, wings collapsed; and forty-one brothers beaming to see one so old escape a cloistered life.

Page 201, mooned: A photo of this toddler is on page 80.

Page 206, sunset: Students had told me all of China ran on one time zone set to Beijing time – hence the 10PM sunset.

Page 209, scriptures: In many Tibetan Buddhist scriptures, extreme sacrifices were rewarded with little poems of wisdom. The following examples were published in *Stories from Dun Huang Buddhist Scripture*, translated by Li Yu-liang and Liang Xiao-peng, Gansu Children Publishing House, 2002, pages 144-145 and 148, respectively:

Those who live will perish,
Those who were high will fall,
Those who join will part,
Those who are will not be at all.

Everything in the world is impermanent
And all living beings are in misery.

Morning mountain range northwest of Beijing

The Buddhist law is open to all
And it is impossible for me to own it.

Page 210, Great Wall: I have since seen photos of the Great Wall at Jiayu-guan that stretch impressively along a nearby ridge, a sandstone version of the walls and watchtowers I visited near Beijing. I feel bad to have missed seeing this section in person. Had I been able to explain to the bus driver my reason for asking, I'm sure he would have provided a fuller explanation.

Page 212, Dickens: Generally speaking, copyright laws weren't enforced in China. *A Tale of Two Cities* had long since passed into the public domain, but the book I read was a photocopied knockoff of the Penguin Classics edition, right down to the copyright page and the off-color Penguin logo on the cover. I also picked up a copy of Chaim Potok's *The Chosen*. Bootlegs of titles like these could be found in most large bookstores.

Several teaching organizations took exception to Chinese institutions' practice of distributing low-cost photocopies of Western textbooks, easily identified by their green covers and thin paper. Prices charged by Western publishers were prohibitive, beyond the budgets of most Chinese students.

Page 213, airline: When I stopped by China Airlines' downtown office to pick up my new tickets, the agent simply crossed out the information on my existing tickets and handwrote the corrections. That didn't strike me as adequate, so I asked him to print new ones. He refused, insisting his corrections would be sufficient.

Lo and behold, I arrived for my connecting flight in Tokyo to discover that Japan Airlines had no record of me. The agent made one fruitless call

Posing

after another about my situation. After an hour, her tone suggested that the airline was simply gifting me a ticket to move me along. I'll never forget her consummate professionalism – so kind, and so absolutely dogged to assist me.

Page 221, graduate program: From a student composition:

Many Chinese students dream of studying abroad, especially to America. If I have a chance to be admitted into a university in America, I'll value the opportunity and study hard than ever. I'll enjoy the good environment for studying. Even though I dislike the stress of studying in school as a student, I'll be glad to make my dream come true.

Page 222, growth: China's economic growth is primarily *urban*, occurring at the expense of rural areas being left behind.

Page 223, recruiting: You can also win high school students over to Chinese by explaining the days of the week and months of the year:

Monday	xing qi yi	"day 1"
Tuesday	xing qi er	"day 2"
Wednesday	xing qi san	"day 3"
Thursday	xing qi si	"day 4"
Friday	xing qi wu	"day 5"
Saturday	xing qi liu	"day 6"
Sunday	xing qi ri	"day sun"
January	yi yue	"1 month"
February	er yue	"2 month"
March	san yue	"3 month"
April	si yue	"4 month"
May	wu yue	"5 month"
June	liu yue	"6 month"
July	qi yue	"7 month"
August	ba yue	"8 month"
September	jiu yue	"9 month"
October	shi yue	"10 month"
November	shi yi yue	"11 month"
December	shi er yue	"12 month"

Page 226, map: This is an altered version of the public domain image "China_blank_map.svg" posted by Joowwww on Wikimedia Commons, August 13, 2008: http://commons.wikimedia.org/wiki/File:China_blank_map.svg.

HEADLINES

CHINA DAILY HEADLINES FROM 1993-1994 provide a glimpse into the national mindset:

ARTS

Arts, culture grow with economic reforms 1/18/94

Li strives to preserve China's musical wealth 1/14/94

Weaving a fashion future 12/17/93

'What's up Doc?': Time to reanimate the cartoon world 12/4/93

Where dining out is a religion 1/23/94

Writers profit from columns to bestsellers 1/13/94

BUSINESS

HK stores making quite a stir 11/6/93

Honesty is the best sales policy 7/16/93

Money-losing State enterprises must shut down 1/14/94

Rules aim to improve free market efficiency 7/30/93

Shoppers call hotline for quality 8/11/93

CRIME & CALAMITY

380 dead in floods since July 8/11/93

Capitol police uncovered 740 major criminal cases 8/11/93

Guangdong courts put 9 to death 12/16/93

Public security reports rise in crime in 1993 1/20/94

Weather disasters exacting heavy toll 7/17/93

CULTURE

China defined by dance 7/16/93

Ethnic languages protected 1/22/94

Life in an 'urban' village 12/16/93

Rules set to protect minority nationalities 10/23/93

EDUCATION

Cheating on tests a problem 12/16/93

Complaints over cost of university education 8/11/93

Don't motivate kids with cash 1/14/94

Plan to wipe out illiteracy by 2000 12/16/93

Project aims to teach children about harsh realities of life 1/22/94

University plan targets nation's top young talent 7/30/93

FAMILY

Children lead parents into age of computers 1/23/94

Children take their parents to court 12/14/93

Not easy being a gifted kid 11/23/93

The trouble with kids today 12/10/93

GROWTH

Balanced growth required in all regions 10/27/93

Fair competition the only way to ensure efficiency 1/13/94

Money fever becomes epidemic in China 7/15/93

Moving on in search of space 12/9/93

Quality of life rising steadily 1/23/94

HEALTH

Fresh strategy aims to clean up pollution 10/23/93

Nation should control sales of tobacco 1/14/94

Navel might be path to easing heart disease 1/18/94

Parasites infect most of nation's population 11/27/93

Pollution crisis can't be ignored 11/27/93

Progress marked in disease control 11/3/93

Watermelons cool down overheated Beijingers 7/30/93

POLITICS

Americans more positive about China 12/4/93

Deng visits Shanghai for Spring Festival 2/12/94

Deng's selected works: Guide to a decade of reform 11/3/93

Government fights to make itself more efficient 1/16/93

Jiang calls for deep study of Deng book 11/3/93

Party accelerates reforms: CPC forges policies for socialist market economy 11/15/93

Readers rush to buy Deng volume 11/3/93

GLOSSARY

FOR HELP WITH PRONUNCIATION, stop by the audible glossary at the website theyearismelledlikemilk.wordpress.com.

〇	一	二	三	四	五	六	七	八	九	十	百
ling	**yi**	**er**	**san**	**si**	**wu**	**liu**	**qi**	**ba**	**jiu**	**shi**	**bai**
0	1	2	3	4	5	6	7	8	9	10	100

¥: symbol for Chinese currency (*yuan*)

baba: father

Badaling: highly trafficked tourist section of the Great Wall

Baishite: ice cream brand in Lanzhou

baozi: round steamed buns filled with meat or vegetables

bei: north

Bei Da: Beijing University, one of China's premier universities (equivalent to Harvard or Yale)

Beijing: China's capital; literally "north capital"

Beijing Linye Daxue: Beijing Forestry University

bizi: nose

bu: no; not

bu chi bai bu chi: "There's no point in not eating."

bu yao: don't want

cha bu duo le: so-so; short of the mark but good enough

Chang Cheng: Great Wall

chi: eat

chong lai ma: "Again?"

Da Bai Tu: Big White Rabbit candy, a creamy toffee

Da Shi Tang: large student canteen

dao: go to

daxue: college; literally "big school"

dong xi: thing; stuff

dui bu qi: I'm sorry; pardon me

duo: many

erduo: ear

FEC: Foreign Exchange Currency, a separate monetary system for foreigners intended to protect the domestic economy (no longer in use)

gan bei: cheers (used to toast at a meal)

gebei: upper arm

gei: give

gong bao ji ding: stir-fried chicken with peanuts and vegetables (also known as Kung Pao Chicken)

gong bao rou ding: stir-fried pork with peanuts and vegetables

gong fu: kung fu

guanxi: relationship, connectedness, "pull"; obligation to repay a favor; access to services, including the ability to grant favors to others

He Bo Sen: "Hobson" transliterated into Mandarin

He Laoshi: Teacher He (my last name in Chinese)

hen: very, much

hen hao: very good

Street in Wudu

huai le: broken

hutong: alleys and courtyards formed by traditional, single-floor brick homes

jian zai: "I'm still here."

jiaozi: dumplings with meat or vegetable filling; could be boiled, steamed or fried

kan: look

kuai: a common word for *yuan* (single unit of Chinese currency), equivalent to the English "buck"

kuai dianr: hurry up

lai zhe: come here

lao jia: excuse me

laoshi: teacher

Lao Wai: foreigner, outsider; "Uncle Outsider" – part of the longer rhyme *Lao Wai hen qi guai* ("Uncle Outsider very strange")

le: marker for completed action, equivalent to past tense

lin: forest

Lin Da: short name for Beijing Linye Daxue ("Forestry University")

Linye Daxue: Forestry University

ma: mother (straight high tone); numb (rising tone); horse (bouncing tone); scold (falling tone); spoken with a neutral tone at the end of a sentence to indicate a question

mai ke: "Mike" transliterated into Mandarin (could mean "mountain range lesson" – a commentary on the workload of my classes?)

Bus terminal in Wudu

mao: ten percent of a yuan; equivalent to a dime (formally known as *jiao*)

mei you: doesn't have; often used as a negative response to a question

mei you guanxi: an attempt to release someone from the obligation to repay a favor; literally "doesn't have guanxi"

mianzibao: I've been unable to obtain a confident translation of this term; perhaps the title of a specific newspaper?

mu: tree

Mutianyu: less-trafficked tourist section of the Great Wall

na ge: that

na shi shen me: "What is that?"

naifen: powdered milk

nan: south

Nanjing: literally "south capital," a historical reference

neige: "that," as in "that word …" – muttered while thinking of the next word to say

ni: you, second person singular

ni chi le ma: "Have you eaten?" – a common greeting

ni men: you, second person plural

Peking Duck: roast duck served in burrito-like pancakes with onions and sauce, a Beijing delicacy

pinyin: phonetic Mandarin written using the Latin alphabet; literally "spell sound"

putonghua: standard speech or accent, based on Beijing's local accent, with

With monks at the Tibetan Buddhist festival

extra R's at the end of some syllables ("dour" instead of "duo")

qing: please

qing gei wo: please give me

qing zhuan: please transfer

ren: person

renmin: people

renminbi: currency of the People's Republic of China; literally "people's money"

sen: forest, wooded

shan: mountain

shen me: what?

shen me yisi: "What does this mean?"

shi: to be

shi bing: soldier

shui: water

si: die (bouncing tone); the number four (falling tone)

sui bian: relaxed, casual

ta: s/he, it, third person singular (gender neutral when spoken)

ta men: they, third person plural

tai: too much

tai gui le: too expensive

waiban: an institution's liaison for foreign experts – arranged accommoda-

Monks with prayer beads

tions, assisted with paperwork, provided oversight, served as tour guide

waiguoren: foreigner, outsider

wei: greeting used when answering the phone

wo: I, me, first person

wo men: we, us, first person plural

Wudaokou: name of the market near Beijing Forestry University

Xi You Ji: *Journey to the West*, a 16th century tale that chronicled a monk and his three bodyguards (including the famous Monkey King) on a westward pilgrimage to bring Buddhist scriptures back to China

xia hai: independent business; literally "fall into the sea"

xian zai: now

Xiangqi: Chinese Chess, similar in concept and strategy to international chess

"Xiao Fang": popular song that depicted a love relationship during the Cultural Revolution

xiao shi: hour

xie xie: thank you

xiong: chest

xiuxi: midafternoon rest, nap

Xizhimen: large northwest intersection on Beijing's second ring road

yao: want

Yihe Yuan: Summer Palace, the lakeside retreat where emperors escaped Beijing's summer heat

Vegetable seller, Xiahe

you: have; often used as an affirmative response to a question

you mei you: literally "have or have not," a common construction for questions, equivalent to "is there a ..." in English

Youyi Hotel: government-run hotel for foreigners; *youyi* meant "friendship"

yuan (¥): 100 fen (pennies) or 10 mao (dimes), equivalent to the term "dollar"; on my arrival, $1 US exchanged for ¥8; on departure the exchange rate was closer to $1 US for ¥12

Yuanming Yuan: Old Summer Palace, former emperor's retreat burned down by British and French forces in 1860

zai jian: goodbye

zai nar: where

zao gao: terrible

zen me yang: "How is it going?"

zhe ge: this

zhe ge duo shao qian: "How much money for this?"

zhe shi: "this is," as in "this is to say ..." – muttered while thinking of the next word to say

zhe shi shen me: "What is this?"

zhen de: really

Zhong Guo: China; literally "center country"

zou ba: "Let's go!"

zuotian: yesterday

Evening harvest

ABOUT THE AUTHOR

MICHAEL W. HOBSON lives with his wife and two sons in Columbia, Maryland, where he promotes literacy as a public school media specialist. His interest in cross-cultural understanding comes from the example of humility and openness seen in Jesus Christ.

Hobson holds a M.A.T. in Secondary English from Johns Hopkins University, and a M.S. in School Library Media from McDaniel College. For this project, however, he returned to his roots: a B.A. in The Writing Seminars from Johns Hopkins University.

This is his first book.

theyearismelledlikemilk.wordpress.com

LaVergne, TN USA
09 September 2010
196491LV00008B/126/P